Understanding Difficult Scriptures in a Healing Way

Matthew Linn
Sheila Fabricant Linn
Dennis Linn

ILLUSTRATIONS BY FRANCISCO MIRANDA

Paulist Press
New York/Mahwah, N.J.

Acknowledgments

We want to thank the following persons for their time and loving care in helping us with the manuscript for this book: Lawrence Boadt, C.S.P., Timothy Friedrichsen, Robert Jewett, Maria Maggi, Jerome Neyrey, S.J., Richard Rohr, O.F.M., John R. Sachs, S.J., Douglas Schoeninger, Walter Wink and Arthur Zannoni.

All scripture quotations are from the New Revised Standard Version, unless otherwise indicated.

Book design by Saija Autrand, Faces Type & Design

IMPRIMI POTEST:
D. Edward Mathie, S.J.
Provincial, Wisconsin Province of the Society of Jesus
September 7, 2000

Library of Congress Cataloging-in-Publication Data
    Linn, Matthew.
        Understanding difficult Scriptures in a healing way / Matthew Linn, Sheila Fabricant
    Linn, Dennis Linn ; illustrations by Francisco Miranda.
            p.   cm.
        Includes bibliographical references.
        ISBN 0-8091-4029-2 (alk. paper)
        1. Bible—Devotional use.   2. Bible—Criticism, interpretation, etc.   3. Spiritual
    life—Catholic Church.   4. Christian life—Catholic authors.   I. Linn, Sheila Fabricant.
    II. Linn, Dennis.   III. Title.

    BS617.8.L56 2001
    220.6—dc21

                                                                                    00-054853

Published by Paulist Press
997 Macarthur Boulevard
Mahwah, New Jersey 07430

www. paulistpress.com

Printed and bound in Mexico

Table of Contents

This book is gratefully dedicated to
Agnes May Linn
and those who lovingly helped care for her:
Mary Ellen DeRosa
Ann Nemanich
Mary Rita Thompson, O.S.M.
Gale Volz, P.B.V.M.

Preface

During a retreat, we typically discuss two or three scripture passages that are "difficult," meaning ones that are often misunderstood in ways that present an unloving, frightening or narrow image of God. At the end of our talk, the most common question we receive goes something like this:

> I like the way you interpret those passages. I've never heard anything like that before, but it makes sense to me and I feel closer to God. Now what do I do with all the other parts of the Bible that scare me? Is there one book I can read that has collected interpretations like yours?

Unfortunately, our answer is "No." Although we do not wish to minimize the help that commentaries and other resources for scripture study can offer us (see Suggested Bibliography), we are not aware of any one book that has addressed all the passages of scripture that are "difficult." Indeed, no scripture scholar could write such a book. There is so much information available today about the origins of the Bible and so many creative possibilities for interpreting that information that a scholar could spend a lifetime on a single passage.

While this book likewise does not claim to address all the difficult passages in scripture, we have collected a few of them, along with interpretations from some of the best scholars, that have been healing for ourselves and our retreatants. Good scholars often disagree, and we have not tried to exhaustively present all the possible interpretations of any given passage.

Our intention is only to give examples of life-giving ways to interpret a few difficult passages, so that our readers know this is possible. More importantly, we have tried to present simple criteria that anyone can use in reading any passage of the Bible, so that we come away feeling closer to God, ourselves, others and the universe. This is our goal because, as we will see, loving connection is the essential theme of the Bible.

Moreover, today many people's spirituality is informed not only by traditional sources of faith but by science as well. Since reason does not contradict faith, we can expect that the findings of science will be consistent with the ultimate truths of the Bible and will expand our understanding of it. Just as Galileo's discoveries about the relationship of the earth to the sun invited us to read Genesis in an expanded way, so the findings of modern science are inviting us to read the entire Bible in an expanded way. And science (particularly physics and cosmology) is telling us that we live in a wholistic universe in which everything is related to everything else—all of it held together by love.

The same Spirit that created and guides the universe also inspired the biblical authors. Therefore, when we read the Bible in ways that enhance our sense of loving connection, we are attuning ourselves to the movement of that Spirit and to the whole course of evolution. How, then, can we find the movement of the Spirit in those scripture passages that do not sound loving?

CHAPTER 1

Scripture Can Be a Temptation

When I (Matt) was in third grade, I was preparing for confession. It was about my fourth confession, and I was looking for a way to lump together my usual sins of complaining or delaying when my parents asked me to take out the garbage, vacuum the floors, wash the dishes after eating sticky macaroni and cheese, make Dennis's bed, pick up Dennis's clothes, and so on. Since I wasn't sure I would remember all these sins, I searched for a word that would summarize them. The word I wanted was *disobedience*, but in third grade I didn't have any words that long in my vocabulary.

In second grade we had learned the Ten Commandments in preparation for first communion and first confession. Since we were told the commandments covered all sin, I knew I would find the right word there. So I started rattling them off. When I got to "Thou shalt not commit adultery," I thought, "Oh, that must be what adultery is. ADULTery must be not obeying ADULTS. Why else would they call it *adultery*?" I didn't know any better because the nun's explanation of adultery was quite vague. We were simply told that adultery was a very big sin. It made your soul turn black, and you would go straight to hell if you got hit by a car. It was such a big sin that most people never did it in their whole life. But here I was in third grade and I had already committed adultery fourteen times in just two weeks. So, I was very careful crossing streets.

Finally Saturday came and I could go to confession. There were long lines for confession, and usually I would just choose the shortest, fastest one. But not this time. The shortest line was always the pastor's because he was hard of hearing. He would ask you to speak so loudly that the whole

church could hear. If he still couldn't hear your sin, he would shout, "WHAT DID YOU SAY? WAS THAT ADULTERY? ADULTERY?" When you came out everyone was looking at you but pretending they weren't. Only those whose hearing was as bad as the pastor's or who had minor sins ever risked getting in his line. You could hear them shouting their tiny sins like, "I said the second decade of the rosary too fast."

Since I didn't want the whole church to know about my adultery, I stood in the assistant pastor's confession line with the real sinners. This line was long, so I had about thirty minutes to plan my strategy. I thought,

> He is a young priest, just ordained. He's probably never heard "adultery fourteen times in two weeks." He might fall right off his chair in shock and then everyone will ask me, "What did you say to him?" I'd better soften the blow and give him the sandwich.

To make the "sandwich," you start with bread (a little sin), quickly tuck in the meat (the big sin) and close with more bread (another little sin that will distract him from the real meat). I thought,

> I need a little sin to start with. Oh, I missed my morning prayers seven times. But he will never pay attention to that. I'd better make it twenty times. (My third grade math wasn't up to calculating that it would be a bit difficult to miss morning prayers twenty times in two weeks.) Then I'll quickly whisper "adultery fourteen times." Finally, I need something little to close with, like "I fought with my brother five times." But I'll make it twenty times so he notices it.

So I entered the confessional and said, "Bless me, Father, for I have sinned. It's been two weeks since my last confession. Since then my sins are: I MISSED MY MORNING PRAYERS TWENTY TIMES. I committed adultery fourteen times. AND I FOUGHT WITH MY BROTHER TWENTY TIMES."

There was a long pause, and I knew I was caught. Finally, after about two eternities, the priest said, "How old are you?"

"I'm in third grade, Father."

"I thought so. I don't think you committed adultery. But even if you did, do you know that Jesus forgives you and loves you more than ever?"

"Yes, Father!" I felt thoroughly cleansed of all my guilt so that I could cross streets again without fear of going to hell if I was hit by a car.

How did I get this way? How did it happen that by age eight I was already so scrupulous and perfectionistic that I thought I would be condemned to hell for the normal behaviors of a child? One source of my problem was that our pastor, Father Doyle (not his real name), preached as often as possible on the scripture, "Be perfect, therefore, as your heavenly Father is perfect" (Matt 5:48). He demanded the kind of perfection he preached about. As altar servers we had to have our folded hands pointed straight up to heaven or he would reach over and push them up. I thought that if my hands weren't straight up, my prayers went a different direction and missed God. Father Doyle would make us publicly repeat a Latin response if we had not said it perfectly. If someone tried to sneak out of church early, he would turn around (his back was to the congregation in those days) and tell them to get back in their pew. He was just as hard on himself and once repeated the words of consecration three times until he was sure it was perfect enough for Jesus to enter the bread. Although I'm sure Father Doyle was only doing what his culture and training had taught him was best for his parishioners, his understanding of Matthew 5:48 tormented me throughout my childhood.

Scripture Scared Me, Too

I (Dennis) also grew up with Father Doyle. The passage that scared me most was the story of the last judgment in Matthew 25:31–46. Whenever Father Doyle waved his arms to show how God would separate the sheep from the goats, he made it sound as if it would be awfully easy to be one of those goats that merited eternal punishment.

What had I done to merit eternal punishment? Like Matt, even as a young child I was already very scrupulous. For example, I thought that every impure thought or sin against sexuality was a mortal sin. The first time I thought I had committed a mortal sin was just before my second-grade dance recital. Four or five of us second graders were doing the Elves' Dance. We had gathered with our mothers in a classmate's home in order to make last-minute alterations in our costumes. At one point, one of the mothers opened the bathroom door, and I saw my classmate, Ann, sitting on the toilet. I had never before seen a girl going to the bathroom. I knew I wasn't supposed to look, and as I kept watching Ann I was sure I was committing a mortal sin.

That night at the dance recital, I couldn't remember any of the dance steps we had practiced for an entire year. I was consumed with terror at having committed a mortal sin and meriting the eternal punishment of hell. This terror pervaded my childhood and adolescence. All girls became for me "occasions of sin." That is why, even as an adolescent, I never dated. Ultimately this fear of hell led me to join the Jesuit order. I entered the Jesuits for many good reasons but also because at that time religious life was seen as the best way to save one's soul, especially a soul as black as Matthew 25 had made me imagine mine to be. Thus, for me, scripture was a grave temptation to unhealthy and self-destructive scrupulosity.

Jesus Was Tempted by Scripture and So Is Our Whole Culture

According to Matthew 4:1–11, Jesus, too, was tempted by scripture.* During the temptations in the desert, Satan quoted scripture (Ps 91:11–12) to invite Jesus to pursue power, honor and riches. Jesus told Satan to stop tempting him with scripture: "Worship the Lord your God and serve only him."

Not only Jesus but our entire culture has been tempted to abusive and unloving practices by scripture. For example, until 1891, official Church statements endorsed slavery. The Church's acceptance of slavery was based upon passages in the Old Testament** (Gen 21:9–10; Exod 20:10, 17) as well as the New Testament: "Slaves obey your earthly masters with fear and trembling, in singleness of heart, as you obey Christ" (Eph 6:5).

The New Testament was commonly interpreted to justify not only slavery but also the persecution of Jews. Based upon Matthew 27:25, "His blood be on us and on our children!", Jews were blamed for Jesus' death (blatantly overlooking the role of the Romans, as well as the fact that Jesus, his family and all his early followers were Jews). Thus, Jews were denied basic rights to land and to practice most professions. In 1442, the Council of Florence proclaimed that Jews who did not enter the Catholic Church would go to hell.

Not only Jews but other Christians, as well, have been persecuted on

---

*A fundamental question in scripture study is the extent to which the words and actions of Jesus as reported in a given passage are historically accurate, and the extent to which they were added later by the biblical authors. We will address this question in Chapter 6. Here, in citing the story of Jesus' temptation, and elsewhere in this book, where we perceive the critical issue as not historicity but rather a simple point about Jesus' basic stance, we will follow the common practice of proceeding as if Jesus did say the words and perform the actions attributed to him.

**Some authors use the terms "Hebrew scriptures" and "Christian scriptures," instead of "Old Testament" and "New Testament," to avoid implying that the New Testament replaces or supersedes the Old. We share this concern but have chosen to use the more traditional nomenclature for the following reasons: (1) using "Christian scriptures" as the equivalent for "New Testament" implies that Christians use only the New Testament rather than the entire Bible; (2) using "Hebrew scriptures" as the equivalent for "Old Testament" is inaccurate, since some Old Testament texts are in Aramaic and others are in Greek (if the Deuterocanonical books are included).

the basis of scripture. For example, during the Reformation, the Inquisition sought out and burned Protestants, who were judged to be heretics. This was justified by John 15:6: "Whoever does not abide in me is thrown away like a branch withers; such branches are gathered, thrown into the fire, and burned."

One area in which the misinterpretation of scripture has been especially common and destructive is the role of women and sexuality in general. For example, a passage commonly cited to support the subordination of women is Genesis 2:18, "Yahweh God said, 'It is not good that the man should be alone. I shall make him a helper'" (New Jerusalem Bible). The word *helper* (sometimes translated as "helpmate"), which is repeated again in verse 20, is from the Hebrew *ʿezer*, and is usually misinterpreted to mean that women are meant to be subordinate to men. However, this word is used a total of ten other times in the Old Testament. In one instance, Isaiah 30:5, the reference is to Egypt, a nation far more powerful than Israel. In the other nine instances, the reference is to God as the helper of Israel (Exod 18:4; Deut 33:7, 26, 29; Pss 33:20; 70:5; 115:9, 10, 11). Thus, contrary to popular thinking, *ʿezer* clearly does not mean a subordinate.

Misinterpretations of both the Old and New Testaments have often degraded women and sexuality in general. As James Fischer writes,

> When the New Testament was translated into Latin the legal viewpoint of Rome started to creep in. In 1 Cor 7:6 Paul, speaking in the tradition of Jewish wisdom, suggested that Christians might abstain from marital intercourse for the purpose of praying, but only for a time. His sentiment read literally: "This I say as a suggestion by way of indulgence . . ." which got translated later into English as "concession." The semitic mind had no idea of suggesting that marital intercourse was in any way indecent. But the Latin suggested that one needed some sort of excuse or permission to enjoy sex. . . . The social conditions influenced interpretation.

One person who contributed to this was St. Jerome, who did an early Latin translation of the New Testament (the Vulgate). Jerome had fled to the desert to avoid sexual temptations. While there, to distract himself from his temptations, he studied all the languages necessary to read original biblical documents (Hebrew, Aramaic, Greek, Chaldean, etc.). With a less than

wholesome attitude toward sexuality, he then began translating the scriptures into Latin. The Vulgate was used as the basis for other biblical translations (including the Douay-Rheims version, the first English translation, used for centuries by Catholics, including Father Doyle).

Finally, in modern times scripture scholars returned to the original documents. Jerome's negative attitude toward sexuality prevailed until Vatican II, in which the Church finally affirmed that sexuality within marriage did not require the excuse of procreation of children but might also be enjoyed to further the relationship between husband and wife.

Good News or Bad News?

This chapter has explored examples of the harm done to us personally and to our culture by scripture. Yet, scripture is intended to be good news. How did the good news of scripture so often get turned into bad news? And how can it get turned back into good news? These will be our questions throughout the rest of this book.

Healing Process

1. Close your eyes and breathe deeply. Ask yourself which passage of scripture is your favorite. For example, which passage of scripture do you return to when you need comfort and reassurance?

2. Read that passage slowly. Close your eyes, place your hand on your heart and continue to breathe deeply, breathing in the comfort and reassurance that you find in this passage. Notice how you feel toward God and how you imagine God feels toward you.

3. Think of a scripture passage that you find difficult—one that puzzles or frightens you.

4. Read that passage slowly. Close your eyes, place your hand on your heart and breathe deeply. Notice how you feel toward God and how you imagine God feels toward you.

5. Note any difference between these two experiences of reading scripture.

CHAPTER 2

Love Is the Criterion

The bad news of Father Doyle's interpretation of the last judgment scene in Matthew 25 scared me (Dennis) so much that I lived a crazy life. As a young adult, much of my energy was devoted to avoiding sexual temptation and thereby eternal punishment. Only when I was called to visit my friend, Bill, in a mental hospital did I realize there must be another way to read the Bible.

When I arrived at the hospital, Bill's hands were chained to his bed and a bandage covered the right side of his face. That morning Bill had tried to gouge out his right eye. When I asked him why, he quoted Matthew 5:29, "If your right eye causes you to sin, tear it out and throw it away; it is better for you to lose one of your members than for your whole body to be thrown into hell."

Everyone knew Bill was crazy for taking the first part of that passage, "If your right eye should cause you to sin, tear it out and throw it away," so literalistically. But I realized that Bill was no more crazy for taking the first part of that passage literalistically than I was for taking the second part literalistically and believing that God would vengefully throw me into hell. Bill was no more crazy than I had been the night of the second-grade dance recital when, after watching Ann in the bathroom, I believed I had committed a mortal sin and God was going to send me to hell.

Bill was the first of several people who gave me the key to turning the bad news of scripture back into good news: knowing that God loves me at least as much as the person who loves me the most. I was the person who loved Bill the most. In the previous ten years, I had visited Bill in thirteen institutions, including city and county jails and federal prisons. Despite the

fact that Bill had lived what might be regarded as an awful life (he was involved in drugs, prostitution and probably murder), and despite the fact that he showed little intention or capacity to change, I knew I would never give up on him.

As I looked at Bill's mutilated face, I knew I could never say to him, "I love you more than you could ever imagine. But you blew it. You have had many chances to repent and change but you haven't changed at all. So, to hell with you." If I couldn't say these things, then God, who loved Bill a whole lot more than I did, couldn't either.*

---

*To summarize Roman Catholic theology on this point, both heaven and hell are possibilities. We know that there are some people in heaven, but we do not know if anyone is in hell. If anyone is in hell it is not because God sent that person there but because he or she chose it. We do not know if anyone has ever made or ever will make such a choice. Karl Rahner, perhaps the greatest theologian of the twentieth century, says that we may hold out the "unshakeable hope" that every single person will be saved. For more on the subject of hell and related questions of free will, and so forth, see our book *Good Goats: Healing Our Image of God* (Mahwah, N.J.: Paulist Press, 1994).

Looking at Bill, I knew that our misunderstanding of scripture had made both of us crazy. Although I couldn't put it into words then, knowing Bill laid the foundation for what has now become my criterion for reading scripture:

> IF ANY INTERPRETATION OF A SCRIPTURE PASSAGE IS NOT CONSISTENT WITH MY LIFE EXPERIENCE OF AUTHENTICALLY GIVING AND RECEIVING LOVE, THEN I AM NOT UNDERSTANDING WHAT GOD WANTS TO SAY TO ME THROUGH THAT PASSAGE.

Love is the criterion. Thus, I knew that even if Jesus did say the words attributed to him in Matthew 5:29, when Bill gouged out his eye he certainly had a wrong understanding of what Jesus really meant. But how could I apply my criterion for reading scripture to Matthew 25:46, the passage that was driving me crazy?

Matthew 25:46 Has a Problem

What drove me crazy about Matthew 25:46 were the words "eternal punishment." Matthew 25:46 is the only passage in all the New Testament where these two words appear together, side by side. If love is indeed the criterion for reading scripture, then a passage in which Jesus threatens eternal punishment poses a problem. Following are some principles that have helped me resolve this problem.

When a Passage Seems Unloving, Compare It with the Rest of Scripture

As Richard Rohr says, the fundamental message of scripture is that God loves us and can be trusted. Through a long and circuitous process of development, the biblical writers moved toward eliminating all violence from God. Thus, in the risen Christ, which is the final biblical revelation of the nature of divine love, we have a totally nonviolent God whose very breath is identified with forgiveness (John 20:22–23). However, to arrive at this point, Rohr says the scripture writers, "took three steps forward and two steps backward." This forward and backward process is one reason why there are so many "difficult" passages in scripture, such as Matthew 25:46. Although such passages may be among the most frequently quoted, they may also represent the "two steps backward."

As usually interpreted, Matthew 25:46 portrays a violent, unloving and untrustworthy God. Similar passages, in which vengeful punishment is attributed to God, occur frequently in Matthew. However, as scripture scholar Walter Wink says,

> The overwhelming number of these passages appear in Matthew, and have no parallel in the other Gospels. Matthew clearly has added them. . . . Matthew adds threats of hellfire, eternal torture, and everlasting punishment that he does not find in his sources. . . .

Given this inconsistency with the other Gospels, we need to ask, what's going on with Matthew? Why does this Gospel so often seem to take "two steps backward"?

Although 25:46 is an exception, most of the threats of "hellfire, eternal torture, and everlasting punishment" in Matthew were aimed at the Pharisees. In the other Gospels, not only are there few threats of punishment but also the passages are seldom addressed to the Pharisees. Why does Matthew's Gospel need to heap vengeance upon the Pharisees?

Scripture scholar Bernard Prusak offers one possible explanation. He suggests that Matthew and his community are simply doing to the Pharisees what the Pharisees did to them. After an unsuccessful revolt against Rome in 70 A.D., the Pharisees believed God was punishing them for defiling their religion by allowing Jewish followers of Jesus to worship in their synagogues.

They decided to put their house in order. Thus, the Pharisees inserted into their synagogue prayers a petition asking that the Jewish followers of Jesus perish. This effectively stopped Jewish Christians from worshiping in the synagogue. These same Christians (members of Matthew's community) responded by adding to their scriptures threats that God would consign the Pharisees to hell (Matt 23:15, 33).

Commenting on the vengeful punishment passages in Matthew's Gospel, Walter Wink says,

> . . . the most frequent deviation in the New Testament itself from Jesus' standard is the lust for punishment of the wicked . . . where the church seeks revenge on its persecutors.

Thus, the vengeful punishment passages that are so prevalent in Matthew's Gospel were probably added by Matthew's community. In fact, they seem to take us far from the historical Jesus and from his message in almost the entire rest of the New Testament.

The most consistent message in the Christian scriptures, the "three steps forward," is unconditional love. Jesus' consistently loving behavior does not match the usual interpretation of the words of Matthew 25:46. In this passage, Jesus tells the apostles that those who do not care for him when he is hungry or thirsty, when he is a stranger or in need of clothing, or when he is sick or in prison will receive eternal punishment. Then, as spiritual writer Susan Mech observes,

> Within forty-eight hours these men will call Jesus a stranger, they will leave him in prison, hungry, sick, thirsty and naked. They will do these things not to "Jesus in one of his disguises," but to Jesus himself, the Jesus that has been with them in person for three years. What is Jesus' response?

Rather than punishing them, the risen Jesus welcomes his followers who had abandoned him during his passion and says he will never abandon them: "I am with you always, yes, to the end of the age" (Matt 28:20).

Something similar happens in the other Gospels. In Luke, Jesus responds with unconditional love not only toward his own followers but also toward the entire crowd who has left him in prison, hungry, thirsty and

naked. His final words from the cross to the crowd, who are apparently still unrepentant, are "Father, forgive them for they do not know what they are doing" (Luke 23:34). In Mark, there is no mention of punishment either. In John 21:9–12, the risen Jesus appears to his apostles by the Sea of Galilee:

> When they had gone ashore, they saw a charcoal fire there, with fish on it, and bread. . . . Jesus said to them, "Come and have breakfast."

As Susan Mech writes,

> Jesus doesn't say, "Here, hop on these coals and begin your eternal punishment." Rather, Jesus says, "Come and have breakfast."

In fact, nowhere in the Gospels do we find a word of vengeance from the risen Jesus. Rather, we find only words of love for the very people who had mistreated him, and the gracious invitation to "Come and have breakfast." Thus, whatever Matthew 25:46 *does* mean, considered in light of the whole of scripture, its seemingly vengeful message does not appear to be what God most wants to say to us.

What Is the Literary Style of a Passage?

The Bible includes many different kinds of literature, ranging from history to poetry. Raymond Brown compares reading the Bible to reading a newspaper. When we pick up the paper, we instinctively adjust ourselves to the type of literature on that particular page. If we are reading the headlines on the front page, we expect that what we read is factually accurate. If we are reading an editorial, we expect personal opinion. If we are reading the advertisements, we know they may be largely exaggeration or even fiction. The Bible includes fiction, history, biography, poetry, etcetera. Much of it is symbolic and therefore multifaceted in its meaning.

Perhaps because they understood this, when the Jewish rabbis studied the Old Testament they were not looking for *the* meaning of a particular passage. Rather, their method was to discuss (and often argue about) each passage, with each rabbi giving his interpretation. These varying points of view were recorded in the Talmud (a collection of Jewish rabbinical interpretations of scripture), and the whole conversation was regarded as part of an ongoing interpretation of the passage.

Different points of view could all be considered part of the rabbinic interpretation of a scripture because of the symbolic nature of much of the biblical literature and because of the multifaceted nature of symbols. Like a good rabbi, Jesus frequently used symbolic language, as in the parables, to speak truths beyond rational understanding. According to scripture scholar Dennis Hamm, Matthew 25 is more a parable than "a straightforward description of how it will be at the end."

Following are two voices that might be included in a conversation about Matthew 25. Both are examples of the symbolic thinking that can enhance our understanding of this passage. The first comes from a very old Roman Catholic nun, and the second from the great theologian, Hans Urs von Balthasar.

We Are All Good Goats

We met the nun while we were guests at her convent several years ago. I (Dennis) gave a homily one morning in which I said that God loves us at least as much as the person who loves us the most, and therefore God would never send us to hell. This nun raised her hand and said, "But what about the story of the sheep and the goats? It says right there that the sheep go to heaven and the goats go to hell."

I responded by asking the whole group, "How many of you, even once in your life, have done what Jesus says at the beginning of that passage and fed a hungry person, clothed a naked person or visited a person in prison?" All the sisters raised their hands. I said, "That's wonderful! You're all sheep." Then I asked, "How many of you, even once in your life, have walked by a hungry person, failed to give clothing to a person who needed it, or not visited someone in prison?" Much more slowly this time, all the sisters raised their hands. I said, "That's too bad. You're all goats."

The sisters looked quite distressed. Then the old nun's hand shot up and she blurted out, "I get it! We're all good goats!" That sister did get it. She understood that one way to interpret Matthew 25 is symbolically. In this sense, heaven and hell are not specific geographical places. Rather, they are symbols for states of being that all of us have experienced. Whenever we have felt alienated, unloved, overwhelmed by shame or helplessly caught in an addiction, we have experienced hell. Hell is alienation. Whenever we have been welcomed home, seen our goodness reflected in the affirming eyes of another or have been loved into recovery, we have experienced heaven. Heaven is union. We've all been in heaven and we've all been in hell. We all have wheat and weeds within us, we're all sheep and we're all goats. Perhaps one meaning of Matthew 25 is that the kingdom of God (heaven) is within us, and we're all good goats.

The Descent into Hell

Since God is love—love that is infinitely beyond all our imaginings—the most loving possible interpretation of any passage will always be the closest to the truth, even if it is not the most common interpretation. Sometimes we find an interpretation of a scripture passage so radically loving that it turns everything else inside out, in the surprising way that is characteristic of the Holy Spirit.

Such is Hans Urs von Balthasar's symbolic understanding of the descent into hell, a doctrine that is relevant for our understanding of Matthew 25:46. As commonly taught, the descent into hell, mentioned in 1 Peter 3:19 ff., referred to Jesus' going to preach to, teach and heal the just souls awaiting redemption. However, the New Jerusalem Bible footnote to 1 Peter 3:19 says that Jesus goes to hell to heal the unrepentant, such as the chained demons mentioned in the Book of Enoch and those in Noah's time who were punished by the flood because they "refused to believe."

Von Balthasar asserts that Jesus' descent into hell, commemorated each Holy Saturday, signifies not a literal trip by Jesus to a geographical place, but rather Jesus' utter solidarity with sinners. As the expression of God's infinitely merciful love for sinners, Jesus identifies completely with them, to the point of dying on the cross as one of them. Seemingly abandoned by God, Jesus cries out, "My God, my God, why have you forsaken me?" (Matt 27:46). In this moment Jesus experiences the "hell" of God's absence more acutely than would be possible for any other person.

Then, on Holy Saturday, Jesus goes to be with sinners in still another way, in what we call his descent into hell. If we define hell as the adamant choice to close one's heart to God, then it would seem that hell is the one place where God cannot be. By going there anyway, Jesus refuses to accept that choice and expresses God's unwillingness to leave us to our own worst selves. Von Balthasar says,

And exactly in that way, he disturbs the absolute loneliness striven for by the sinner: the sinner, who wants to be "damned" apart from God, finds God again in his loneliness, but God in the absolute weakness of love who unfathomably in the period of nontime enters into solidarity with those damning themselves. The words of the Psalm, "If I make my bed in the netherworld, thou art there" (Ps 139:8), thereby take on a totally new meaning.

Perhaps an image that can help us understand Jesus' descent into hell is the behavior of loving friends and family, who will not leave a suicidal person to his or her worst self. They will do everything possible to enter into that person's hell in order to intervene and stop that person from taking his or her own life. In a similar way, Jesus' descent into hell is his refusal to accept our choice of destruction. Holy Saturday proclaims that Jesus' mission is to demonstrate solidarity with us by even, if necessary, descending into our hell and being with us there until his healing presence renews us enough to rise with him on Easter.

Consider the following story:

A man who was entirely careless of spiritual things died and went to Hell. And he was much missed on earth by his old friends. His business manager went down to the gates of Hell to see if there were any chance of bringing him back. But, though he pleaded for the gates to be opened, the iron bars never yielded. His cricket captain went also and besought Satan to let him out just for the remainder of the season. But there was no response. His minister went also and argued, saying, "He was not altogether bad. Let him have another chance. Let him out just this once." Many other friends of his went also and pleaded with Satan saying, "Let him out. Let him out. Let him out." But when his mother came, she spoke no word of his release. Quietly, and with a strange catch in her voice, she said to Satan, *"Let me in."* And immediately the great doors swung open upon their hinges. For love goes down through the gates of Hell and there redeems the damned.

How can Matthew 25:46 be interpreted in a way that is consistent with Jesus' descent into hell and with the kind of love that impels a mother to go to hell to be with her son?

When the Passage Doesn't Seem Loving, Check the Translation

One reason that Jesus' words in Matthew 25:46 seem inconsistent with this kind of love is because, according to scripture scholar William Barclay, the words *eternal* and *punishment* are mistranslated. The Greek word we translate as "eternal" is *aionios*. Barclay says that *aionios* does not mean an infinite quantity of time as we know it. Rather, *aionios* refers to a different *quality* of time, God's time rather than human time. The Greek word we translate as "punishment" is *kolasis*. According to Barclay, *kolasis* was used to refer to the pruning of trees for therapeutic reasons, to help them grow better. If Barclay is correct, a better translation of the words *aionios* and *kolasis*, rather than "eternal punishment," would be something like, "healing in God's time." It does seem that is what the apostles, who acted like goats, experienced. As they smelled the fish roasting on the coals and received Jesus' warm welcome, "Come and have breakfast," the apostles began receiving "healing in God's time."

The fact that individual passages may be poorly translated or may have more than one possible translation is all the more reason why, as we have already said, we can find the essence of Jesus' message on any topic only by considering the whole of scripture. Consistent with the descent into hell, the New Testament as a whole affirms God's desire to bring "healing in God's time" to everyone. See, for example, John 3:17, 12:32 and 12:47b; Romans 5:12–21 and 11:30–32; 1 Corinthians 15:22 and 28; Ephesians 1:10; Philippians 2:10–11; Colossians 1:19–20; 1 Thessalonians 5:9; 1 Timothy 2:3–6 and 4:10; Titus 2:11; Hebrews 2:9; 1 John 2:2; and Revelations 5:13.

When We Are Most in Touch with Our Life Experience of Giving and Receiving Love, We Are Most Likely to Find the Message of Love in Scripture

Since our fundamental criterion is love, we are most likely to understand scripture correctly when we ourselves are most in touch with love. For example, we (Dennis and Matt) once met a wealthy doctor, Jorge, in the Philippines. Jorge had sold most of what he owned and used the money to build a clinic in a barrio of cardboard houses. A common problem among the people had been intestinal parasites, caused by going barefoot on the

unsanitary ground. As he took us from home to home and introduced us to his friends, several times he pointed to someone's feet and said, "He is wearing my shoes." Finally, we asked Jorge, "How many pairs of shoes did you own?" He said,

> I used to have nearly fifty pairs of shoes. I also was depressed all the time. Now, I have two pairs of shoes and all these people that I love are wearing the rest of them. And, I am almost always happy.

When Jorge fell in love with the people, he discovered one of the possible meanings of Matthew 25: When we don't share we will feel like hell.

Another example of how being in a state of love helps us find the loving message of scripture comes from William Wilson, a former Trappist. As a monk, he had learned how to pray with a high degree of detachment. But when he became a father, all this changed:

> . . . when I (any parent) pray(s) for my child's eternal happiness and ful-
> fillment, I pray for it absolutely. I cannot find it in myself to pray in a
> surrendered spirit. A negative answer is unthinkable and absolutely unac-
> ceptable.
>
> I leave God no other choice in the matter. In my prayer I absolutely
> demand of God that God give happiness to my son for eternity. . . .
>
> I am so extreme about this that God knows it would be over between
> God and me if my son were to be lost. It is as if I were saying to God:

"Look, you either bring my son to eternal life or just forget about any relationship with me." I just do not have a "conditional" or "surrendered" prayer within me about my son's final blessedness.

Not very pious, but I do not think it is incorrect. I now believe the passion a parent feels for the ultimate well-being of the child is a revelation of, and a participation in, the passion God has for every child of God. Which would mean that these feelings and this absolute will, expressed in my imperious prayer, are fully in harmony with the will of God.

As William Wilson says, when we are most in touch with our capacity for unconditional love, we glimpse most clearly the unconditional love of God that is the overriding message of scripture. His passion for his child's ultimate well-being is a participation in this unconditional, healing love of God.

What, then, does Matthew 25:46 mean? Taking into account Barclay's translation of the words *aionios* and *kolasis*, one likely meaning is that, like William Wilson's passion for the ultimate well-being of his child, God has a passion to heal all God's children, and this will happen in God's time.

Perhaps we can further understand what this passage might mean by remembering that things look different from our point of view than from God's. From our point of view, when we ignore those who are hungry or naked or in prison, we feel like hell. This was Jorge's experience. As long as he hoarded shoes and ignored the needs of the poor, he was depressed. Consider also Peter, who left Jesus hungry, naked and in prison. He felt so awful that, "he went out and wept bitterly" (Matt 26:75).

Human beings are made for love and connection. Research confirms that even very young children, if they have not been wounded, are naturally altruistic. For example, beginning when our (Dennis and Sheila's) son, John, was one year old, if he heard another baby cry he himself would cry. Then he would point to the other baby and say, "Give John's milk."

Thus, perhaps the harsh judgment in Matthew 25:46 is one we bring upon ourselves. When we deny our true nature and ignore those in need, we suffer terribly and feel like hell. If we have done this long enough, we may become overwhelmed by our own suffering and alienation. Then we may fall into the addictive substitutes for inner peace used so commonly in our culture to numb out pain. Yet, from God's point of view, as in the case of

Jorge and Peter, God's only desire is to restore us to ourselves and bring us healing in God's time.

In What Sense Is the Bible Inerrant (Without Error)?

Because the theme of healing love for everyone is so central to the Bible, it is *this* salvific truth that comprises the inerrancy of the Bible, rather than other forms of inerrancy commonly attributed to scripture. Regarding inerrancy, church historian Richard Smith writes,

> The basic problem is easy to state: The allegedly inerrant Bible contains statements that in any other document would be regarded as erroneous; . . . (1) biblical self-contradictions, e.g., Noah's flood lasting forty days and nights in Gn 7:17, but 150 days in Gn 7:24; (2) errors in natural science, e.g., the universe enwrapped in waters held back by a solid bell-shaped barrier called the firmament (Gn 1:6–8); (3) errors in history, e.g., the inaccuracies of Dn 5; and (4) moral errors, for example . . . total destruction of an enemy people or group, considered as carrying out of the will of Yahweh (Jos 11:14–15).

Thus, the Bible is not inerrant scientifically, historically, or even morally. As Richard Rohr says, the Bible is not about morality, but about ontology. *Ontology* refers to being. The Bible is about our being, about who we are: daughters and sons of God. Thus, as scripture scholar Eugene LaVerdiere says, it *is* inerrant in its fundamental assertion of "God's intention to save all human beings and all that that statement implies. God has promised salvation to humanity, and God is true to that promise."

It is God's love that saves us. Authentic love does hold us accountable and at times may invite us to change our lives, as in the case of Jorge. But authentic love will never be vengeful nor condemning and will always reach out to offer healing. The theme of this chapter is that such love is the criterion for understanding Matthew 25:46 or any other passage of scripture. If an interpretation of scripture does not enhance our appreciation of God's salvific love, meaning God's intention to save all human beings, then we have not understood that scripture at its deepest and most inerrant level. Jesus himself used this same criterion of love to interpret scripture, as we will discuss in the following chapter.

Healing Process

1. Close your eyes and breathe deeply. Think of the person who loves you the most. (This can be a person who has died, since the deceased continue to love us through the Communion of Saints.) Place your hand on your heart and breathe in that person's love for you.

2. Ask yourself which scripture passage most closely communicates to you the depth of love you feel from this person. Breathe in that love, knowing that God loves you at least as much as the person who loves you the most.

3. Now think of a difficult scripture passage—a passage you find puzzling or frightening. Ask yourself how the person who loves you the most or God would explain this passage so that it conveys love to you. If you are not satisfied with the explanation for the passage, give yourself permission to temporarily set it aside until it does convey love to you. Once again, breathe in how God loves you at least as much as the person who loves you the most.

CHAPTER 3

Jesus' Criterion
for Reading Scripture

As an adult, I (Matt) studied the passage that had caused me so much trouble as a child, "Be perfect, therefore, as your heavenly Father is perfect" (Matt 5:48). I discovered that Jesus could never have said these words. Jesus spoke Aramaic and there is no word in Aramaic for "perfect." The only ancient manuscripts of the Gospel of Matthew that we have are in Greek. As Walter Wink explains,

> . . . Jesus could not have said, "Be perfect." There was no such word, or even concept, in Aramaic or Hebrew. And for good reason. The Second Commandment had forbidden the making of graven images (Exod. 20: 4). Israel consequently never developed the visual arts. The word used by Matthew *teleios*, was however, a Greek aesthetic term. It described the perfect geometric form, or the perfect sculpture.

Thus, scripture scholarship makes it clear that our understanding of *perfect* was not what Jesus meant in Matthew 5:48. But few of us are scripture scholars. How, then, can we increase our chances of discovering the real meaning of a passage? A difficult passage may be illuminated and even corrected by the rest of scripture. Thus, we can read the rest of the passage (Matt 5:43–48) for which "Be perfect . . ." (v. 48) is the conclusion.

> "You have heard that it was said, 'You shall love your neighbor and hate your enemy.' But I say to you: Love your enemies and pray for those who

persecute you, so that you may be children of your Father in heaven; for he makes his sun to rise on the evil and on the good, and sends rain on the righteous and on the unrighteous. For if you love those who love you, what reward do you have? Do not even the tax collectors do the same? And if you greet only your brothers and sisters, what more are you doing than others? Do not even the Gentiles do the same? Be perfect, therefore, as your heavenly Father is perfect."

The context makes it clear that Jesus is not asking us to be perfect in the sense of never making a mistake. Rather, Jesus is asking us to love as God does, forgiving even those who make mistakes (the "evil" and the "unrighteous"). The parallel passage in Luke 6:36 substitutes for "Be perfect" what Jesus more likely said, "Be compassionate as your Father is compassionate" (New Jerusalem Bible). Walter Wink writes,

Placed in its context within the rest of the paragraph, Jesus' saying about behaving like God becomes abundantly clear. We are not to be perfect, but like God, all-encompassing, loving even those who have least claim or right to our love. Even toward enemies we are to be indiscriminate, all-inclusive, forgiving, understanding. We are to regard the enemy as beloved of God every bit as much as we. We are to be compassionate, as God is compassionate.

Jesus' Norm for Judging All of Scripture

Sometimes, even reading the context of a passage and parallel passages doesn't help us. What do we do then? In such cases, we can rely on Matthew 22:34–40, where Matthew's Jesus seems to give us a norm for judging all our scripture interpretations:

When the Pharisees heard that he had silenced the Sadducees, they gathered together, and one of them, a lawyer, asked him a question to test him. "Teacher, which commandment in the law is the greatest?" He said to him, "'You shall love the Lord your God with all your heart, and with all your soul, and with all your mind.' This is the greatest and first commandment. And a second is like it: 'You shall love your neighbor as yourself.' On these two commandments hang all the Law and the Prophets."

When Jesus says, "On these two commandments hang all the Law and the Prophets," he seems to be saying that these two commandments are the norm for interpreting all of scripture. For the Sadducees, the law (the first five books of the Bible, known as the Torah in Hebrew or the Pentateuch in Greek) was their normative scripture. The Pharisees added the prophets as also normative. Thus "The Law and the Prophets" was a shorthand way in Jesus' culture to speak of the scriptures (Matt 5:17). For example, the scribes who studied and taught all the scriptures were referred to as "teachers of the Law" and not "teachers of the scriptures." Thus, in Matthew 22:34–40 Jesus seems to have given love as the norm for interpreting scripture, whether one was the conservative Sadducee or the more liberal Pharisee who included the prophets as well.

Jesus himself interpreted scripture according to this same norm. He supported the requirements of the law, but only to the extent that he could do so in a way that was consistent with love. Thus, when referring to the regulations regarding the sabbath, temple worship or divorce, Jesus consistently quoted the more loving traditions of Genesis and the prophets, rather than the more legalistic parts of Exodus, Deuteronomy or Leviticus. Scripture scholar Jerome Neyrey writes,

> As regards the Sabbath, appeal is made to the scriptural example of David, the great saint and king. David, a non-priest, entered priestly space and ate food reserved exclusively for priests (Mark 2:23–28/1 Sam 21:1–6). . . . When the temple is cleansed (Mark 11:17), it is proclaimed not as a place of sacrifice for Jews only, but as (1) "a house of prayer," (2) "for all the nations." Isa 56:7 is promoted over the cultic legislation of Exodus and Leviticus. When divorce is discussed, the original law of God in Gen 1–2 is preferred to the law of Moses which this mere man wrote "because of the hardness of your hearts" (Mark 10:4–5/Deut 24:1–3).

However, in the case of the laws concerning with whom one could eat, Jesus apparently could not find traditions that were sufficiently loving, and so he created his own. Thus, he ignored the prohibitions regarding table fellowship and ate with Gentiles (Mark 8:1–10) and sinners (Mark 2:15), as well as with the lame, blind and maimed (Luke 14:13). Jesus ate with everyone, because this was the way in which he could give and receive the most love.

Jesus not only taught the scriptures, but even more importantly he taught us a process for relating to scripture. His ultimate criterion was not the words that are written but rather what was most loving. Paul follows Jesus' example, to the extent of contradicting Jesus' own teachings. For example, many scripture scholars agree that the absolute prohibition of divorce found in Luke 16:18 and Mark 10:11 is among the most authentic sayings of Jesus. In 1 Corinthians 7:10, Paul acknowledges Jesus' prohibition of divorce: "To the married I give this command—not I but the Lord—that the wife should not separate from her husband" (1 Cor 7:10). He then goes on to allow an exception, in the case of marriage to an unbeliever, presumably because he believes this would be most loving for his community (1 Cor 7:12–16). He acknowledges openly that he is disagreeing with Jesus, saying, "This is from me and not from the Lord."

Not only Paul, but also Matthew gives an exception—unchastity—to Jesus' prohibition of divorce (Matt 5:32; 19:9). Joseph Fitzmyer says that Matthew's exception was "scarcely part of the otherwise authentic saying of Jesus prohibiting . . . divorce absolutely, without any exceptions." Paul and Matthew felt free to make exceptions to what Jesus *said* because they were following Jesus' *process* for interpreting the scriptures: Follow what is consistent with your life experience of giving and receiving authentic love and don't get hung up on the rest. Thus, Paul and Matthew follow Jesus' spirit of love rather than his actual words.

Therefore, the question we need to ask of any scriptural interpretation is whether it leads us to give and receive more love with God, our neighbor and ourselves. If not, we are not hearing the good news that God is speaking to us. For example, if an interpretation of "Be perfect, therefore, as your heavenly father is perfect" leads us to a legalistic perfectionism, in which we lack mercy toward ourselves or others who are imperfect, we are not understanding God's message.

This is the case even if our interpretation is taken word for word from the scriptures. Satan tempted Jesus in the desert by quoting the scriptures word for word. Our interpretation of scripture should always result in growth in love for God, others, ourselves and the universe. When it doesn't, scripture is a temptation rather than good news.

Healing Process

1. Close your eyes, place your hand on your heart and breathe deeply. Think of a scripture passage that you find difficult.

2. Tell God how your present interpretation of this passage would make it more difficult for you to love God, others, yourself and the universe.

3. Listen for God's response.

CHAPTER 4

Jesus Was a
Conscientious Objector

If it were immediately evident how to interpret the words attributed to Jesus in scripture in a loving way, there would be no need to write this book. However, some of the words attributed to Jesus don't sound at all loving. Even allowing that some of these words may be mistranslated or that some may not be Jesus' words at all but rather additions by the early Christian community, we are still left with many other instances where Jesus doesn't sound at all loving. What do we do then? One barrier to understanding Jesus comes from misunderstanding the historical and cultural context, meaning the world in which he lived.

I (Dennis) studied Spanish in American schools for many years. But it was only when the three of us went to language school in Bolivia and immersed ourselves in Latin American culture that I began to understand the Hispanic world from the inside. Similarly, we have all studied scripture in American theological schools, but it was only when we (Dennis and Sheila) studied scripture in Jerusalem that we began to understand Jesus' world from the inside.

We studied at an institute located on the border between Israel and the occupied territories, on the road to Hebron. We arrived just after the Hebron massacre, in which a Jewish soldier massacred many Palestinians as they prayed in their mosque. Even though the culprit was a Jewish soldier, for weeks afterward the Israeli military would not allow Palestinians to leave their homes in the occupied territories. Since many of them had jobs in

Jerusalem, this meant they had no way to support their families. We often saw them hiding in the bushes on the grounds of the place where we lived, trying to sneak into Jerusalem to work or visit relatives. As we returned from our morning jog, they would ask us if there were any Israeli soldiers nearby or if it was safe to come out. We, who were strangers in a foreign country, had more freedom to move about than people whose ancestors had lived in this land for thousands of years.

The political situation in Israel is extremely complicated, and each side has arguments to justify its behavior. On the one hand, Jewish Israelis have suffered such hideous violence that their desire to protect themselves is understandable. Yet, it also seems true that the Palestinians are an oppressed people living under an Israeli domination system. Studying scripture in this environment helped us grasp that Jesus, too, was part of an oppressed

people. In fact, the religious and political domination system of his time ultimately put Jesus to death.

From their enslavement in Egypt during the time of Moses through the Babylonian Exile and the Roman occupation of Israel in the time of Jesus, the Jewish people spent much of their history under the domination of one or another more powerful nation. The moments they celebrated were moments of liberation. For example, two of the most significant Jewish feasts were (and still are) Passover and Hanukkah. Hanukkah celebrated the victory of the Maccabees over Syria. Passover celebrated the Jewish people's exodus from Egypt. Every Passover the people read the scriptures about their exodus and how they had resisted Egypt's domination. Many Jewish revolts, including those in Jesus' time, took place on Passover. According to John's Gospel, Jesus himself was put to death during Passover.

Palm Sunday in America vs. Palm Sunday in Jerusalem

When I (Dennis) celebrated Palm Sunday in Jerusalem and then recalled how I celebrated Palm Sunday growing up, I realized how far I had been from understanding Jesus' world. During my childhood, on Palm Sunday our family would join the rest of the congregation as they processed out of the church and around our neighborhood. At the front of the procession were the Knights of Columbus carrying the American flag, and the rest of us followed waving our palms. When we returned to church for the conclusion of Mass, we prayed three Hail Marys for the conversion of Russia (as we did at every daily Mass). To be a "good Catholic" meant flag-waving and praying for "our" guys to win and the "other" guys to lose, even as Church officials blessed the U.S. war machine. I assumed that Jesus, too, was a flag-waver and a supporter of the American domination system.

Like my childhood experience of Palm Sunday, the Palm Sunday procession we attended in Jerusalem was politically charged. Because the Israelis feared that the Hebron massacre might trigger a Palestinian uprising during the Palm Sunday procession, only one or two busloads of Palestinian Christians were permitted to enter Jerusalem to participate in the celebration. Most visible to us during the procession were Israeli tanks, and it seemed to us that the procession included nearly as many soldiers as worshipers.

Our militant experience of Palm Sunday in Jerusalem was not unlike what Jesus experienced. Palms were already an important political symbol for the Jewish people. As scripture scholar Dennis Hamm writes,

> Palm branches reminded people of the days of the Maccabees, nearly two centuries before Christ. After Judas Maccabeus and his guerrilla fighters took back the temple from the Syrian oppressor, Antiochus IV, the people brought palm branches to the temple on the occasion of its rededication (the event still celebrated at Hanukkah). Ever since that event, palm branches had been a sign of Jewish nationalism.
>
> . . . some Galilean coins struck around A.D. 24. . . . bear the image of the emperor Tiberius Caesar, but the coins have been restruck with the image of a palm smack across the face of the emperor—a political statement if there ever was one.

For the Jews in Jesus' time, palms were the equivalent of flag-waving and blessing the war machine. When the people welcomed Jesus with palms, they were communicating their desire that he lead a military revolt against the Roman occupation and that he become a political and military leader in the tradition of Judas Maccabeus.

When, instead of getting on a warhorse, Jesus mounted a lowly donkey, the Gospel of John reports the people's disappointment (John 12:12–19). (Although all the Gospels have Jesus mounting a donkey, only in John's Gospel are palms mentioned.) Jesus' response to flag-waving Jewish nationalism was his refusal to bless anyone's war machine. Instead, he taught (as we will see below) conscientious objection.

Although Jesus did challenge every domination system of his time, including Jewish nationalism, he did so in a way that advocated conscientious objection through nonviolence. The followers of Jesus understood this message so well that, according to Walter Wink,

> No one disagrees that the early Church denounced war. For the first three centuries Christians were virtually unanimous in denouncing Christian participation in battle. In fact, in the first three centuries . . . there is not a single record of a Christian violently resisting the Empire.

Unlike the comfortable world of my childhood in which our church and our country were always right, during his humble entry into Jerusalem Jesus proclaimed that he would not be a flag-waver and that every domination system must be questioned.

Palm Sunday in Jerusalem helped me realize that I cannot fully understand the meaning of many of Jesus' words and actions unless I understand his nonviolent resistance toward the domination system of his time. Following are two examples of passages that make sense only in this light.

A Story of Conscientious Objection: The Parable of the Pounds

Just before Jesus mounts a donkey instead of a warhorse, he tells the Parable of the Pounds in Luke 19:11–27, often identified with the Parable of the Talents in Matthew 25:14–30. As you read the parable, you might ask yourself two questions: (1) Which servant is the hero of the story? and (2) Do you like the nobleman?

> . . . he went on to tell a parable, because he was near Jerusalem, and because they supposed that the kingdom of God was to appear immediately. So, he said, "A nobleman went to a distant country to get royal power for himself and then return. He summoned ten of his slaves, and gave them ten pounds, and said to them, 'Do business with these until I come back.' But the citizens of his country hated him and sent a delegation after him, saying, 'We do not want this man to rule over us.' When he returned, having received royal power, he ordered these slaves, to whom he had given the money, to be summoned so that he might find out what they had gained by trading. The first came forward and said, 'Lord, your pound has made ten more pounds.' He said to him, 'Well done, good slave! Because you have been trustworthy in a very small thing, take charge of ten cities.' Then the second came, saying, 'Lord, your pound has made five pounds.' He said to him, 'And you, rule over five cities.' Then the other came, saying, 'Lord, here is your pound. I wrapped it up in a piece of cloth, for I was afraid of you, because you are a harsh man; you take what you did not deposit, and reap what you did not sow.' He said to him, 'I will judge you by your own words, you

wicked slave! You knew, did you, that I was a harsh man, taking what I did not deposit and reaping what I did not sow? Why then did you not put my money into the bank? Then when I returned, I could have collected it with interest.' He said to the bystanders, 'Take the pound from him and give it to the one who has ten pounds.' (And they said to him, 'Lord, he has ten pounds!') 'I tell you, to all those who have, more will be given; but from those who have nothing, even what they have will be taken away. But as for these enemies of mine who did not want me to be king over them—bring them here and slaughter them in my presence.'"

If asked which servant was the hero of this story, most people respond, "The servant that brought back ten pounds." When asked if they like the man of noble birth, people usually say, "No." Some don't like him because he is a murderer, others because he steals from the poor and gives to the rich, others because he is vengeful and hard-hearted. In Mexico, when we asked our retreat group if they liked him, they shouted, "No! He is like our government!"

The problem is that most Christians have heard a sermon on this passage (or the similar parable in Matthew 25:14–30), where the emphasis has been on using our gifts or talents well. In such sermons we are told that God will reward us, too, just as the nobleman did the servant who returned with ten pounds, if we take risks to serve God generously. However, God will punish us if we hide our gifts. This interpretation reinforces our cultural values of hard work, earning our own way, the poor are just lazy, and wealth is God's blessing. These values are projected onto God. However, such an interpretation presents God as no better than the nobleman whom everyone hates.

At least two things ought to warn us that such homilies are far from the meaning Jesus intended. First, when God is identified with the nobleman, God is presented as less loving than the person who loves us the most. Secondly (and many Americans would miss this), God is presented as encouraging the investment of money in order to earn interest. Jews called this practice usury. In Jesus' time, the Jewish community's list of the seven most despised professions included usurers, who were denied all civil and religious rights. Usury was not only denounced by Jesus but, even as late as 1569, three papal bulls unequivocally condemned it.

What (and whom), then, is this parable about? The Jerusalem Bible footnote for this passage suggests one possible explanation. According to the footnote, the cruel nobleman, far from representing God, probably represents the Judean ethnarch Archelaus. After the death of Herod the Great in 4 B.C., his son, Archelaus, went to Rome to receive his inheritance. There, he was crowned ethnarch of Judea. On his return from Rome, the hated Archelaus put to death a delegation of fifty Jews who tried to block him from being confirmed as king. (In Matthew 2:22, even Mary and Joseph, as they returned from Egypt, were warned in a dream not to return to Archelaus's Judean territory.)

The hero, then, seems to be the servant who keeps Archelaus's money in a piece of cloth rather than investing it to earn more money to support Archelaus's tyranny. The others all became part of the ethnarch's repressive government as they receive cities to oversee. Archelaus committed so many atrocities that in 6 A.D. Caesar Augustus deposed him for fear the Jews would riot. Thus, if this interpretation is correct, the parable is really saying that we are to stand up and resist an abusive system at all costs.

Jesus told this parable just before mounting his donkey on his way to Jerusalem and his passion. Like the parable's just servant, Jesus was sentenced to death by the domination system that he constantly resisted. As a resister to both religious and political domination, he was charged with wanting to destroy the temple and make himself a king. Thus, one possible interpretation of the Parable of the Pounds is that if we become a conscientious objector and confront an abusive system, like the just servant and Jesus himself, we will risk the cross.

The cross itself became a symbol of conscientious objection. The Roman Empire terrorized its colonized subjects by threatening death on a cross to any rebel. For instance, as Jesus told his listeners about Archelaus, they would know that what made his tyranny possible was three Roman legions that, on Archelaus's behalf, had quelled a Jewish rebellion by crucifying two thousand rebels outside Jerusalem's walls. Jesus' conscientious objection merited him that same kind of death. However, Jesus' resurrection proclaimed that the power of imperial violence did not have the last word. The Roman Empire's means of terror, the cross, became the early Christians' symbol of a faith that declared, "Stand up and resist an abusive system at all costs."

If it is true that Jesus was a conscientious objector, then we can better understand why he spoke in parables. Several years ago, we (Matt and Dennis) went to Korea shortly after the Kyongju massacre in which the Korean military murdered as many as twenty thousand government protesters. Our sponsors asked us to travel to the major cities, including Kyongju, to help people heal this hurt. Wherever we traveled, the Korean police followed us. They wanted to make sure that we never mentioned the Kyongju massacre. If we had, they would have arrested us and our sponsors.

So, we spent two weeks speaking in parables. For example, Matt would speak about the five stages of forgiveness that he had gone through in forgiving a student who attacked him. Then we would lead people through a process to forgive someone who had hurt them. Tens of thousands of people attended those conferences. Most wept as they began the process of healing the hurt caused by the Kyongju massacre, despite the fact that we never once mentioned the massacre itself. Like ourselves in Korea, Jesus was also watched. In order to survive and still confront the domination system of his time, he, too, often had to speak in parables.

Another Story of Conscientious Objection: Turn the Other Cheek

I (Sheila) did not grow up with the kinds of distortions of scripture or of the message of Jesus that Denny and Matt grew up with, because I did not grow up hearing about Jesus at all. I come from a Jewish family, and what I did grow up with were the effects of many centuries of religious violence—violence that was often justified by the way that scripture was interpreted.

For example, just after I became a Christian I went to visit my father's four sisters. The three oldest sisters and my father were born in Poland, and the youngest sister, Anne, was born in America. I saw Anne first. She said,

> I love you and I accept your decision to become a Christian, but I want you to know that my sisters are very upset about this. At least, when you go to see them, don't wear a cross, because that will really frighten them.

Then Anne told me that when her sisters were children in Poland, Easter Sunday was a holiday for the Polish soldiers. For their recreation, the Polish soldiers would go out and hunt Jews with bayonets. Thus, my aunts' memories of Easter were of hiding in the basement from the Polish soldiers. That's what the cross meant to them.

The justification for the Polish soldiers' behavior (and for much other cruelty to Jews in Poland and elsewhere) was an interpretation of scripture: that the Jews killed Jesus. Thus, Jews have been the victims of many centuries of religious violence. As often happens when people have been victimized one time too many, in modern Israel we have seen Jews finally explode and rise up in violence themselves. Many Israelis honestly believe this violence is justifiable because of the need for self-defense.

This cycle of victimization and then explosion in the name of self-defense is consistent with the assumption throughout Western culture that we have only two choices when it comes to violence: Either give it or passively take it, either kill or be killed, either hit somebody else or be hit ourselves. Much of this assumption is based on a misunderstanding of what God is really saying to us about violence and how to respond to it. Sometimes we use scripture to justify violence, as has happened in modern Israel, where Jewish settlers cite passages from the Old Testament regarding the gift of the promised land and its defense. Other times we use scripture to prove that the "Christian" thing to do is not defend ourselves and just let ourselves be abused.

Jesus' attitude toward violence was very different. A critical passage is Matthew 5:38–42, where it says,

> "You have heard that it was said, 'An eye for an eye and a tooth for a tooth.' But I say to you, Do not resist an evildoer. But if anyone strikes you on the right cheek, turn the other also; and if anyone wants to sue you and take your coat, give your cloak as well; and if anyone forces you to go one mile, go also the second mile."

When I have read this passage to retreat groups and asked if they like it, most people say, "No!" If I ask, "Why not?", typical answers include,

"It tells us to act like a doormat."

"It encourages abuse."

"It takes away your dignity and your power to protect yourself."

If I ask, "How many of you actually live this way? How many of you, if someone stole your car, would give that person the keys to your house?", most people admit that they would not. These answers are clues that something may be wrong with our usual interpretation of this passage.

If we want to understand this passage, we must first ask ourselves, does God condone violence? Specifically, does God want us to let other people hit us, take things from us and force us to do things we don't want to do? The passage seems to say, "Yes." Yet, according to Walter Wink, something *is* wrong with the way we have interpreted this. His analysis of Matthew 5:38–42 is virtually the opposite of its usual interpretation.

Turn the Other Cheek

The passage begins with, "You have heard that it was said, 'An eye for an eye and a tooth for a tooth.' But I say to you, Do not resist an evildoer." Let us set this aside temporarily, and go on to verse 39b: "But if anyone strikes you on the right cheek, turn the other also." If we are to understand this correctly, the first question we need to ask is why Jesus specified the right cheek. He did so for cultural reasons known to his listeners.

First of all, Jesus' listeners knew that the left hand was regarded as unclean. Thus, if I were to hit you on the right cheek, I would have to use my right hand. The only way I could comfortably do this if you were facing me would be if I hit you with the back of my hand. Everyone listening to Jesus knew that hitting another person with the back of the hand was a gesture that had a specific meaning in their culture and was used only in specific situations. Only people with more power would backhand people with less power. For example, masters would backhand slaves, Romans would backhand Jews, husbands would backhand wives and parents would backhand children. In Jesus' culture, slaves, Jews, wives and children had no power.

The purpose of hitting another in this way was not to physically harm that person. Rather, the purpose was humiliation. Backhanding another was intended to communicate, "You stay in your place, which is beneath me." This is a situation of social and emotional violence, more than physical violence.

Now, imagine that you are still facing me and you turn your left cheek to me. Unless I contort my arm into a pretzel, I can no longer backhand you. If I strike you again, I will have to either use a fist or the front of my hand. Everyone listening to Jesus knew that this was a gesture used only between *equals*. Thus, by turning your left cheek you are saying to me, "I am not beneath you and you may not humiliate me. I may not be able to stop you from hitting me, but you can't take away my dignity."

According to Walter Wink, this is an example of "Jesus' Third Way" of creative nonviolence. Jesus is telling us that when we are in a situation of violence, we should neither passively suffer abuse nor should we retaliate in a way that escalates the cycle of violence. Instead, Jesus encourages us to find a creative third way in which we retain our dignity. This third way reveals the truth of the situation and ideally even calls our oppressor to conversion, whether or not he or she accepts the invitation.

Give Away Your Undergarment

The next part of the passage says, "If anyone wants to sue you and take your coat, give your cloak as well." The context in this case is that in Jesus' time there was a highly exploitive economic system, in which the Romans were taxing the Jews. The poor had to take out loans to pay the taxes. Most of the people were poor, and the whole purpose of this system was to force them to default on loans so the rich could seize their land.

A creditor could demand that a debtor give collateral on a loan. The debtor might give his house or his cow or some other possession as collateral. When the debtor had nothing left, the creditor would demand the debtor's outer garment as collateral. We know that this was a common practice among Jews because there are passages in Exodus (22:25–27) and Deuteronomy (24:10–13, 17) that refer to it. These passages say that if you've taken someone's outer garment as collateral you have to give it back at night because it's all that person has to sleep in during the cold desert nights. Thus, demanding a debtor's outer garment was a familiar symbol of oppression in Jesus' time. Our modern expression, "taking the shirt off someone's back," expresses how degrading it was.

The setting is a courtroom and a creditor is demanding that you, a poor person, turn over your outer garment. Jesus says, "Here's what you do when you're in a situation like this. Your creditor is demanding your outer garment (*himation*)? Give him your undergarment (*chiton*), too."* In Jesus' culture, a chiton might be worn by itself in public without embarrassment. However, since nothing was worn underneath it, giving it away would be as if, in our culture, you gave away your underwear. If you gave away your underwear in our culture, or if you gave away your chiton in Jesus' culture, the result would be the same: you would be naked.

In Jesus' culture, it was not so scandalous to be naked yourself as it was to look at another person naked. As your creditor looks at you naked, he must now experience the humiliation he has tried to bring upon you. You

---

*In this passage from Matthew, it is actually the chiton, rather than the himation, that is demanded. However, in the parallel passage in Luke 6:29–30 the order is reversed so that what is demanded is the himation. The Jewish practice of giving the outer garment as collateral, referred to in Exodus 22:25–27, makes it evident that Luke's order is correct.

have said to him, in effect: "Look at the situation you yourself have created, a situation that degrades all of us." According to Walter Wink,

> The creditor is revealed to be not a legitimate moneylender but a party to the reduction of an entire social class to landlessness, destitution, and abasement. This unmasking is not simply punitive, therefore; it offers the creditor a chance to see, perhaps for the first time in his life, what his practices cause, and to repent.

Once again you have regained your dignity by taking back your power to choose your own response, all without violence. Moreover, you have offered your oppressor an opportunity for conversion.

Go the Second Mile

The passage continues with, "if anyone forces you to go one mile, go also the second mile." In Palestine in the time of Jesus, Roman occupying soldiers could require the local inhabitants to carry their packs. The packs weighed sixty to eighty-five pounds, and Roman subjects hated this practice of forced labor. The Romans wanted to exploit the people, but they were shrewd enough to want to avoid riots. Thus, they passed laws limiting the amount of forced labor that could be required. In the case of packs, a Roman soldier could force a local civilian to carry it only one mile. If the soldier demanded more, he himself could be punished.

Imagine, then, that you are a poor Jew and a Roman soldier grabs you and demands that you carry his pack. You know how far a mile is because the Roman roads were marked. You come to the mile marker and instead of returning the pack, you cheerfully keep on carrying it, assuring the Roman soldier that you wouldn't want *him* to have do it. He is now thoroughly confused and afraid he himself will be punished. Imagine him pleading with you to give back his pack!

Once again you have regained your dignity in an abusive situation. You have exercised your power to choose your own response and you have refused to behave as a victim, all without striking the soldier or otherwise getting caught up in the cycle of violence.

Find a Creative Nonviolent Way to Resist

Let's return then to verse 39a, "Do not resist an evildoer." The word that we translate as "resist" is *antistenai* in Greek. It means to rise up in a military sense—it's a very strong word that implies violence. Thus, when Jesus tells us not to *antistenai*, he is telling us not to take an eye for an eye, that is, not to hit back or otherwise return violence in kind. Then he goes on to give three situations of abuse and oppression that were typical in his time, and in each case he makes it clear that we are not to be passive victims, either.

Instead, when someone tries to abuse or humiliate us, Jesus invites us to find a creative, nonviolent way to resist. Even in situations of injustice that we cannot fully change, we can at least maintain our power to choose our response. As Gandhi said, "The first principle of nonviolent action is that of noncooperation with everything humiliating." Jesus' message is similar and goes something like this:

> Break the cycle of violence and begin by refusing to let yourself be abused. Do it as best you can under the circumstances, even if only by standing up straight and speaking the truth as they lead you to the cross. Sometimes that's all you can do—but do something. Don't just take it.

Because the historical and cultural context of Matthew 5:38–42 has not been familiar to most readers, it has commonly been interpreted in a way that easily leads to a tolerance of abuse. This passage is an excellent example of how difficult it can be for us to understand scripture in a loving way if we do not understand its context. When a scripture contradicts our life experience of giving and receiving love, we may need a good commentary to help us understand the historical and cultural context.

Our knowledge of the context in which the scriptures were written continues to grow, as in the case of Walter Wink's relatively recent original research on Matthew 5:38–42. Therefore, if even commentaries don't help us, we may need to wait for further research and for the Spirit to enlighten us. However long this process takes, we never need to simply accept an interpretation of scripture that encourages abuse toward ourselves or others.

Healing Process

1. Close your eyes, place your hand on your heart and breathe deeply. Think of a difficult scripture, especially one that has been interpreted in ways that encourage abusive behavior toward yourself or others.

2. Recall a time when you were a conscientious objector—a time when you nonviolently resisted injustice.

3. As a conscientious objector, how would you interpret this passage? You may wish to ask Jesus, Gandhi, Joan of Arc, Martin Luther King, Rosa Parks, Dorothy Day, Nelson Mandela or another highly regarded conscientious objector to help you.

CHAPTER 5

Scripture Grows, Just Like People Do

Several years ago, we (Dennis and Sheila) were studying in Jerusalem during Holy Week. We attended a talk on the relationship between Passover and Easter, given by a rabbi and a priest. The rabbi described God's treatment of the Egyptians. I (Dennis) asked, "Do you really believe that God sent plagues on the Egyptian people? That seems to encourage an image of God as vengeful and punitive." The rabbi responded that this is what the Bible says, and so he did believe that God directly caused the suffering of all the Egyptian people as punishment for their treatment of the Israelites. The priest, on the other hand, spoke of Jesus' death on the cross and his words, "Father, forgive them; they do not know what they are doing," as an example of God's forgiving love for sinners.

In Exodus, the Egyptian people made a mistake, God warned them, they did it again, and God sent plagues. In the Gospels, the people made a mistake, God warned them, they did it again and Jesus died on the cross as one of them. As Richard Rohr puts it, the tendency in the Old Testament, based upon aspects of the Deuteronomic Code, was to expect punishment (rather than healing) for the unrepentant sinner, as in the case of the Egyptians. This paradigm had the following movement: I sin, God punishes me, I repent, God loves and rewards me. Jesus ultimately turns this paradigm upside down, as when he forgives his unrepentant tormentors from the cross. Here, the movement is: I sin, I am unrepentant, I am loved and rewarded by God, this heals me so I can repent.

Lest what we have said be taken as lacking in reverence for the Jewish tradition, within that tradition a similar degree of universal compassion can be found. For example, in Isaiah 54:9, God is presented as one who will never again punish sin. Instead God will heal the hard-hearted sinner by being excessive to the excessive degree, by "astounding these people with prodigies and wonders" (Isa 29:14, New Jerusalem Bible). Similarly, in a commentary on the story of the Israelites crossing the Red Sea, God reproaches those who want to celebrate the death of the Egyptians by saying, "The work of my hands is drowning in the sea, and you desire to sing a song." Moreover, although Jesus was criticized for healing on the sabbath, many interpreters of Jewish law would applaud him. They include the rabbis who interpreted Leviticus 18:5, in which God instructs the Israelites that by keeping the commandments they shall live, as a warning *not to die* by the commandments. Thus the rabbis affirmed that ritual observance of the sabbath was less important than preserving life.

In fact, the Hebrew and Christian traditions are not so disparate as might seem from the story of the rabbi and the priest. Jesus was a good Jew whose ethic of love was profoundly rooted in the Old Testament. He consistently drew out the essentially loving message of the Old Testament, focusing on what Richard Rohr calls the "three steps forward" and ignoring the "two steps backward." For example, the law of love given by Jesus in Matthew 22:34–40 that seems to be his norm for interpreting all of scripture comes from Deuteronomy 6:5 and Leviticus 19:18.

The Bible is a process of growth and development in an increasingly mature understanding of the nature of love (and therefore of God), in which violence and self-interest diminish and universal compassion increases. The Bible reflects the developmental process of every human life and of the human community as a whole. We (Dennis and Sheila) watch our three-year-old son's increasing awareness of the needs of other people and his growing capacity to, for example, wait until Mama is off the phone when he wants attention. Our society as a whole has moved from a world in which only white males had rights to one in which all people are recognized as having equal dignity and value. The Christian community now denounces slavery, even though the Bible endorses it and even though Catholic doctrine accepted it until Leo XIII's correction in *Rerum Novarum* in 1891.

The Bible reveals a similar process of growth and development. It is inspired in the overall *movement* it reveals, rather than in all the stops and steps backward along the way. Just as we (Dennis and Matt) gradually grew out of Father Doyle's legalistic image of God into one that is increasingly universal and compassionate, so the Bible moves in this same direction.

Jesus Understood Scripture Developmentally

Jesus related to scripture in a way that is consistent with a developmental understanding of it. For example, in Luke 4:14–19, Jesus, in the Nazareth synagogue, proclaimed his own mission using the words of Isaiah 61:1–2. But why, after he proclaimed his mission, was the whole audience filled with indignation to the point of wanting to hurl Jesus over the edge of the mountain (Luke 4:30)? One reason is that Jesus would not heal those in his own countryside who would not accept him as a prophet. Scripture scholar Robert Jewett suggests a second reason that is often overlooked.

Jewett points out that some Jewish listeners wanted the Messiah to be vengeful to the Romans, to the Sidonians, to the Syrians—to all but themselves. But in quoting Isaiah, Jesus skipped the sentence in 61:2, which speaks of God's vengeance on enemies, and instead declared that God's "favor" rested on all—Romans, Sidonians and Syrians alike (Luke 4:26–27). Jesus angered his Jewish listeners because he was proclaiming the end of vengeful punishment and the reign of a Messiah whose "favor" shines on the just and the unjust.

When Jesus proclaimed an end to the vengeful, violent punishment of one's enemies, he was going against a central theme of the Hebrew Bible. Walter Wink cites Raymund Schwager, who

> . . . points out that there are six hundred passages of explicit violence in the Hebrew Bible, one thousand verses where God's own violent actions of punishment are described, a hundred passages where Yahweh expressly commands others to kill people, and several stories where God kills or tries to kill for no apparent reason (e.g., Ex. 4:24–26). Violence, Schwager concludes, is easily the most often mentioned activity and central theme of the Hebrew Bible.

Although not everyone might agree that violence is the *central theme* of the Old Testament, scripture scholar Robert Jewett agrees that it is a prominent theme. He says that the Nazareth congregation's hoped-for redemption, which included revenge on their enemies, was not just particular to Isaiah 61:2, but was a "major strand of Old Testament religion." Thus when Jesus went against the literalistic interpretation of scripture by leaving out Isaiah 61:2 regarding God's vengeance, and declared instead a year of favor to the Romans, Sidonians and Syrians, the Jewish proponents of the vengeance tradition were so angered that they wanted to hurl him off the mountain.

Jesus was always inviting his listeners to grow beyond a literalistic interpretation of scripture. Often Jesus tried to heal on the sabbath or touch a leper or forgive someone. But the priests, scribes and Pharisees would forbid Jesus to do these things because they interpreted literalistically the vengeful punishment passages of their Bibles that spelled out the consequences of such "illegal" actions.

For example, in the story of the adulterous woman (John 8:2–12), the scribes and Pharisees want to stone her to death. They justify themselves by telling Jesus, "Now in the law Moses commanded us to stone such women" (John 8:5). They are referring to the law of Moses (Deut 22:20; Lev 20:10), which says that God orders the vengeful punishment of stoning to death an adulterous woman. If Jesus, like the Pharisees and scribes, believed such passages fully expressed God's will, he too would have had to join them in stoning the adulterous woman. When he invited the scribes and Pharisees to put down their stones, he was inviting them to set aside a literalistic interpretation of the vengeful punishment passages of the Bible in favor of a more developed and compassionate understanding of the will of God.

Be Holy as God Is Holy vs. Be Compassionate as God Is Compassionate

The developmental movement within the Bible might be summarized as a movement from be holy as God is holy (Lev 11:44) to be compassionate as God is compassionate (Luke 6:36). In the priestly tradition (upheld by the Pharisees), holiness meant living by the "holiness code," found in

Leviticus 17–26. Holiness consisted in living according to an elaborate system of purity laws. Sinners were those who did not obey these laws. Thus, to put it in a somewhat caricatured way, according to this tradition God is presented as a critical parent whose primary concern is that the children keep the house clean.

In the later, prophetic tradition of the Old Testament and in the teachings of Jesus in the New Testament, there is a consistent movement toward compassion as the criterion of holiness, rather than ritual purity (e.g., Hos 6:6/Matt 9:13; Isa 58:1–12; Exod 33:19). Sinners are those who fail to show compassion to others. God is presented as a loving parent who wants the children to treat one another right.

Perhaps this shift, from purity to compassion, is why, according to Walter Wink, Matthew 5:44–45 was the most quoted scripture verse during the first four centuries of Christianity:

> But I say to you, Love your enemies and pray for those who persecute you, so that you may be children of your Father in heaven; for He makes his sun rise on the evil and on the good, and sends rain on the righteous and on the unrighteous.

This passage represents the achievement of the highest level of human development that we know: the capacity to love unconditionally, as God loves, including even our enemies. In this, the Bible has come a long way from the "total destruction of an enemy people or group, considered as carrying out of the will of Yahweh" (Josh 11:14–15).

📖 Healing Process

1. Close your eyes, place your hand on your heart and breathe deeply. Think of a scripture passage that at one time was difficult for you, but that you now find a source of comfort and consolation.

2. Give thanks for the experiences, interior growth, new information, etcetera that have helped you change your understanding of this passage.

3. Hear God speak the words of the passage to you and breathe deeply, breathing in God's love for you.

CHAPTER 6

Who's In and Who's Out

The capacity for unconditional love described in Matthew 5:44–45 rests upon a critical question: who's in and who's out? This was the most difficult question for the Church in the first century of its history (and still is today). If we understand how the early Church and the biblical writers struggled with this question, we can better understand some of the more confusing and difficult passages in scripture. Perhaps a story of how our family has struggled with deciding who's in and who's out can help us understand the early Church's struggle.

A Personal Story

I (Dennis) remember a conversation that my father had forty years ago with his friend, Alex. Alex also belonged to Father Doyle's parish. Father Doyle had heard that Alex's son, George, was going to marry a Protestant. Father Doyle had reminded Alex that there was no salvation outside the Roman Catholic Church and so George's marriage to a Protestant put George's whole salvation in question. George was breaking Church law by consenting to be married by a Protestant minister and in a Protestant church. It was already obvious that George's fiancée was having a terrible influence on him.

Thus, Father Doyle had laid down the law. Under no circumstances was Alex, my father or anyone else in either family allowed to attend George's wedding. Alex was hoping that my father could think of someone more

understanding with whom he could talk. We were hoping, too—we all liked George, especially since he had taught us younger kids to play croquet.

However, my father assured Alex that this was an extremely dangerous situation and it would be unthinkable to attend George's wedding. No member of our family or of Alex's family attended. In fact, we didn't see much of George until years later when my father called to tell him that Alex was dying. George and his wife were still angry about how they had been treated and wouldn't come (although they did finally arrive in time for the funeral).

Today, I am sure that my father would regret what he told Alex. I know this because of a conversation my father had with our Presbyterian pastor friend, Joe. Joe was staying in my parents' home. As he and my father walked over to our parish church on Sunday morning, Joe asked my father if he could receive communion. My father answered, "Do whatever you believe is right." So, Joe went to communion.

Later, having heard about this from Joe, and feeling surprised by how my rather rigidly Roman Catholic father had responded, I had the following conversation with my father, "Dad, when you arrived at the church did you pick up a leaflet missal for both you and Joe?"

"Yes."

"And Dad, what does the Roman Catholic bishops' statement on the back of every leaflet missal say about Protestants receiving communion?"

"It says that if you believe it's the body and blood of Christ, then you should receive."

"Is that what the bishops' statement says?"

"Not exactly."

"What does it say, Dad?"

"It says that communion is a sign of unity and that unless you are in union with Rome and the hierarchy, you should not receive."

"So why did you knowingly disobey what the bishops told you and allow a Protestant pastor to receive communion with you?"

My father looked scared, as if he had been accused of a serious crime. Finally, in desperation, he blurted out, "I did what Jesus would have done!"

My Father Had Two Jesuses and
So Did the Gospel of Matthew

Although the issue was the same (the treatment of Protestants according to Roman Catholic Church law), my father responded very differently to
Joe than he had to Alex. What is surprising is that my father could find support in his favorite Gospel, Matthew, for what he had done with Alex. He
could also find support in Matthew's Gospel for what he did forty years later
with Joe. This is because, according to scripture scholar Jerome Neyrey,
Matthew's Gospel has at least two different authors, with very different attitudes about who's in and who's out.*

These two authors wrote up to forty years apart. The earlier author,
whom we will call Early Matthew, portrays a Jesus who acted like Father
Doyle. This Jesus lived in an insular Jewish community whose members
believed that because they obeyed the letter of the law, they were the only
ones saved. The later writer, whom we will call Final Matthew, portrays
a Jesus who treated everyone in the inclusive way that my father treated
Joe.** This Jesus would have been at home at a Protestant, Jewish or even a
Buddhist wedding.

That two such different portrayals of Jesus survived in the same Gospel
might surprise us. But, as scripture scholar Raymond Brown states, the
writer(s) of each Gospel made "no attempt to report with simple, uncolored
factuality what Jesus had said and done." Rather, as Jerome Neyrey says, the

---

*In what follows we will describe the different attitudes of the two authors, according to
the work of scripture scholar Jerome Neyrey. Note that Neyrey's explanation of the ori-
gin of Jesus' harsh sayings to the Pharisees in Matthew is different from Bernard Prusak's
explanation, given in chapter 2. Both are excellent, highly regarded scholars. The difference between them is an example of how no one theory of the origins of scripture has all
the answers.

**According to Jerome Neyrey, the Gospel of Matthew relies upon three main sources. The
source we are calling Early Matthew was shaped around what is commonly referred to by
scholars as the "Q" tradition. The second source is the Gospel of Mark. The third source
is the material added by the final editor of the Gospel of Matthew, who combined his
material with the Gospel of Mark and Q. We call this final editor Final Matthew. Scholars
estimate that Q and the final editor wrote from twenty to forty years apart. Neyrey dates
Early Matthew as approximately 30 to 60 A.D., and Final Matthew as 80 to 85 A.D.

Gospels are "human attempts to portray a Jesus who reflects their concerns and values and social experience." Just as Father Doyle tried to portray a Jesus that would be pastorally meaningful to Alex and my father's generation, so too did the Gospel writers. Father Doyle's insular Jesus, though not without shortcomings, provided a tight community and a lot of safety for my parents, who, like many Roman Catholics prior to the election of John F. Kennedy as president, were looked at with suspicion and often experienced prejudice.

After John Kennedy's election, my parents' generation felt safer, and my father could gradually set aside Father Doyle's insular Jesus and open himself to Vatican II's more inclusive Jesus, who would welcome an "outsider" like Joe. As with Father Doyle or Vatican II, Early and Final Matthew's portrayal of Jesus were pastorally meaningful attempts to convey the salvific truth that the "situation of their churches" most needed to hear.

> The sacred authors wrote the Gospels, selecting some things from the many which had been handed on by word of mouth or in writing, reducing some of them to a synthesis, explicating some things in view of the situation of their churches. . . .

The Jesus of Early Matthew

If forty years ago, Father Doyle and his parish were insular, Early Matthew's portrayal of Jesus and his community was no different. His Jesus lived in a community made up only of Jews (Matt 10:6). Not only were Gentiles, sinners and tax collectors excluded by the Jesus of Early Matthew, but even most practicing Jews did not qualify. Only observant Jews willing to keep all 613 precepts of the law were welcome (Matt 5:17). This Jesus viewed scribes, Pharisees and other Jews harshly because they were not rigorous enough in keeping the law (Matt 5:20). Just as Alex cut himself off from his own son, Jesus recommended banning anyone who persisted in breaking the law (Matt 18:17). Like Father Doyle, Early Matthew's Jesus preached that there was no salvation outside his community. He and his community were the few who traveled through the "narrow gate" (Matt 7:13–14).

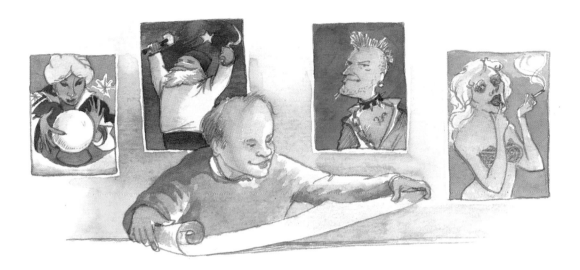

Early Matthew was basically a collection of sayings attributed to Jesus, correctly or incorrectly recalled by his listeners. Final Matthew included not only these sayings but also miracle stories whose basic thrust is the healing of all people from illnesses and endless stories of Jesus welcoming and eating with sinners (Matt 4:23; 9:10). Thus, Final Matthew portrays a very different Jesus. This Jesus lived in a community that was open to everyone: Jews, pagans, sinners and even tax collectors (Matt 9:9). Like my father who upheld Roman Catholic law but could make an exception for Joe regarding table fellowship at Eucharist, this Jesus was a supporter of Jewish law but would make exceptions regarding such things as table fellowship (Matt 9:10–13). In fact, for Final Matthew's community, the symbol for their new relationship with this more inclusive Jesus was Eucharist, a covenant signed with the blood of Jesus (Matt 26:28).

Just as forty years had radically changed my father, so had forty years radically changed the community out of which the final version of Matthew's Gospel emerged. Early Matthew's community had developed sufficiently that they could welcome and celebrate Final Matthew's portrayal of a more inclusive Jesus every time they celebrated Eucharist. Thus, just as there is development within the Old Testament and from the Old Testament to the New Testament in the direction of universal love, so too, in any given book of the Bible there may be similar development.

📖 Healing Process

1. Close your eyes and breathe deeply. Recall a situation in which a scripture passage was used to justify excluding someone, such as a person of another faith, a person with differing political beliefs, a homosexual or lesbian, a woman who wanted to use her gifts, etcetera.

2. Ask Final Matthew how he would rewrite or explain that passage.

3. Place your hand on your heart and breathe in Jesus' unconditional, universal love.

CHAPTER 7

Fundamentalism and the Most Important Meeting in the History of the Church

The struggle regarding who's in and who's out was not only central to the formation of the Gospel of Matthew, but was also the central struggle of first-century Christianity. It was this struggle that necessitated calling the Council of Jerusalem in 49 A.D., which scripture scholar Raymond Brown says,

> . . . may be judged as the most important meeting ever held in the history of Christianity, for implicitly the Jerusalem conference (Acts 15:4–29) decided that the following of Jesus would move beyond Judaism and become a separate religion reaching to the ends of the earth.

In other words, the Council of Jerusalem was the turning point in deciding that not just circumcised Jews were in. Rather, everyone (including Gentiles) was invited to come in.

The Council was called because the early Church was divided. According to scriptural accounts, on one side was the Circumcision Party, composed of Jewish Christians, "insisting that the pagans should be circumcised and instructed to keep the Law of Moses" (Acts 15:5). Opposed to them were the Gentile Christians, led by Paul, who sought freedom from the ritual laws, which they found a burden rather than a way to love. Paul brought with him to the Council the uncircumcised Gentile, Titus, as an example of

a person who was clearly following Jesus yet did not obey all the Mosaic laws. Peter supported Paul and spoke up against a literalistic and legalistic interpretation of the scriptures. From his own experience in Caesarea, Peter knew that God had already accepted uncircumcised Gentiles like Cornelius and his entire household. Peter said,

> And God, who knows the human heart, testified to them [the Gentiles] by giving them the Holy Spirit, just as he did to us; and in cleansing their hearts by faith he has made no distinction between them and us. Now therefore why are you putting God to the test by placing on the neck of the disciples a yoke that neither our ancestors nor we have been able to bear? (Acts 15:8–10)

Peter was then backed by James, who argued that welcoming uncircumcised Gentiles was not against the whole of scripture, since Amos 9:11–12 says pagans will come to the Lord. As the leader of the Jerusalem community, James ruled to drop circumcision and much of the law as requirements for entrance into the community:

> Therefore I have reached the decision that we should not trouble those Gentiles who are turning to God but we should write to them to abstain only from things polluted by idols and from fornication and from whatever has been strangled and from blood. (Acts 15:19–20)

Eventually even three of James's four prohibitions (things polluted by idols, whatever has been strangled and blood) were dropped, because they were deemed to be unnecessary burdens for the Gentile Christians who became the majority.

Because a core issue of the Council of Jerusalem was how to interpret the scriptures of the time with their legal requirements, the Council provides us with a model for reading the Bible today. The story of the Council is the story of a dialogue between the scriptures and the movement of the Spirit in the life of the community. Critical moments in this dialogue are: (1) Peter and Paul's reflection upon their own lived experience; (2) the promulgation by James of a tradition that tries to integrate the essential, loving message of scripture with the movement of the Spirit at the time; and

(3) willingness to later modify even this tradition when aspects of it eventually prove to be burdensome and an impediment to loving unity.

Fundamentalism and the Council of Jerusalem

The conflict at the Council of Jerusalem between Paul's Gentiles and the Circumcision Party is in many ways parallel to the modern struggle between a fundamentalist and a contextual or Catholic view of scripture.* The Circumcision Party advocated a literalistic interpretation of the law of Moses that required circumcision (Acts 15:5). Although we have no record in the scriptures of how the Circumcision Party developed their argument, we might guess that they quoted the law of circumcision in Leviticus 12:3 and perhaps even gave the history of how circumcision was a sign of the covenant with Abraham (Gen 17:10 ff.). Maybe they finished by arguing that Jesus, who followed these same scriptures and was himself circumcised (Luke 2:12), never gave any authorization for such a radical departure from the law.

On the other hand, Paul's group probably would have won right away if he could have said, "Jesus told us that we should admit the Gentiles without circumcision." However, Paul could not use that argument because the historical Jesus probably never encountered Paul's situation. Jesus never thought of himself as founding a new religion outside the parameters of Judaism.

Paul would have to agree with the Circumcision Party that the law advocated circumcision and that Jesus, "born under the law" (Gal 4:4), was indeed circumcised. But he would disagree that scripture, or even in this case the example of Jesus, should have the final word. For both Paul and Peter, the central evidence to be considered was how the Spirit was continuing to reveal itself through the life experiences of their community. Thus Peter recalled Cornelius and Paul brought Titus as examples of how the Spirit had worked in the lives of these two uncircumcised Gentiles.

---

*In this context, *Catholic* does not refer to membership in the Roman Catholic Church. Rather, it is a wider term that is applicable to Anglicans/Episcopalians and members of other denominations as well as to Roman Catholics, whose approach to scripture includes an appreciation for its historical/cultural/literary context. Conversely, there are many individual Roman Catholics whose approach to the Bible is fundamentalist (and thus contrary to official Roman Catholic teaching).

A fundamentalist interpretation of scripture would probably use many of the same arguments that the Circumcision Party used. Fundamentalism holds that the Bible is primary, "the only necessary source for teaching about Christ and Christian living." This total reliance on the Bible rests upon a literal understanding of God's authorship, almost to the point that the words themselves come from God and are only written down by a passive human being. Since God knows all things, not only is the Bible free from error, but it also contains all the answers anyone would ever need. Therefore, when a problem arises, the appropriate question is, "Which Bible verse will take care of it?" The answer for the Circumcision Party was the law of Moses, Leviticus 12:3.

On the other hand, a Catholic interpretation of scripture would follow more closely the example of Peter and Paul and the Council of Jerusalem. After all, if the Bible provided all the answers, why call a council that focused on listening to the lived experience of its participants? Thus, a Catholic perspective does not rely solely on the Bible, but rather on the dialogue between the Bible and the Church's evolving tradition. Tradition is informed by but not limited to the Bible. As theologian Richard McBrien says, tradition is,

> . . . the whole process by which the Church "hands on" (the literal meaning of the word "tradition") its faith to each new generation. This handing on occurs through preaching, catechesis, teaching, devotions, gestures (e.g., the sign of the cross), doctrines, and indeed the Bible itself.

Preaching, catechesis, teaching and such require reflection upon scripture in light of each generation's life experience. This reflective process is what Paul did for his generation at the Council of Jerusalem.

The Catholic approach trusts God's living relationship with people like Cornelius, Peter, Paul, Titus and James. When James finally did quote scripture regarding the circumcision decision (Acts 16:16–18), he did so only after listening to Peter and Paul's testimonies about how the Spirit had worked with the people in their communities. The scripture that James used (Amos 9:11–12) says nothing directly for or against circumcision. Rather, it affirms the salvific truth of what Peter and Paul's communities had experienced: that God wants to save everyone, including the pagans.

The Catholic approach to the Bible is grounded in its understanding of authorship of the Bible. According to Richard Smith, the early theologians, such as Clement of Alexandria, spoke of God as the author of scripture not in the sense that God was the "literary cause of the biblical books." Rather, "author" meant that God is the source or cause of the plan of salvation revealed in the Bible. Thus, God's role as author guarantees salvific truth (e.g., that God indeed longs for the salvation of all people, such as Paul's Gentiles). However, God's role does not guarantee historical, scientific or even moral truth. Truth in these areas cannot be guaranteed because the Catholic approach takes into account the humanity of the writers. Human authors are limited by the tradition(s) and people from whom they receive their material and the audiences they are addressing, as well as by personality, culture, historical circumstances, education, personal experience of God and so forth. Thus, Paul pleaded that certain parts of scripture regarding circumcision were meant for a specific time and culture and were not applicable to his situation.

The Catholic approach bears in mind that the final gospel documents were written at least forty to sixty years after the death and resurrection of Jesus. Since (according to 95 percent of current critical scholarship) none of the writers were eyewitnesses of what Jesus said or did, their accounts came not directly from Jesus but rather from the traditions of various communities.* Each generation changed, developed and modified these traditions, as in the case of Early Matthew and Final Matthew.

Added to this is the common practice among ancient historians and biographers of inventing words for their characters to speak. In this way, those ideas that the storytellers regarded as most important could be expressed, even if they could not recall their characters actually saying such things. This practice was not regarded as dishonest, and it was common even among historians such as Herodotus and Thucydides, as well as the authors of the Bible. Thus, as already mentioned, Raymond Brown says the gospel writers made "no attempt to report with simple, uncolored factuality what Jesus had said and done."

---

*Realizing that the various books of the Bible involve several layers of tradition helps us understand why the Catholic approach emphasizes tradition. As McBrien says, "Scripture is itself a product of Tradition. It is not as if you first have Scripture and then you have Tradition (which is among other things, the Church's subsequent reflection on Scripture). Tradition comes before and during, and not just after, the writing of Sacred Scripture."

All this accounts for some of the seemingly contradictory statements in the Bible. Because so much adaptation occurred, the gospel writers were often trying to put together very different accounts of what Jesus said or did. For instance, regarding the question the Jerusalem Council was considering, in Matthew 10:5 Jesus tells the twelve apostles to "Go nowhere among the Gentiles," whereas in Matthew 28:19, Jesus says, "Go therefore and make disciples of all nations."

Such contradictions need not trouble us if we understand, as the Jerusalem Council did, that the Bible is not primarily a rule of life. As the National Conference of Catholic Bishops asserts,

> We observed in Biblical Fundamentalism an effort to try to find in the Bible all the direct answers for living—though the Bible itself nowhere claims such authority.

The Bible was not intended to provide ready-made answers for unforeseeable theological and moral issues that would arise in subsequent centuries.

As Raymond Brown says, "God chose to deal with such subsequent problems not by overriding all the human limitations of the biblical writers but by supplying a Spirit that is a living aid in ongoing interpretation."

If, at the Council of Jerusalem, the fundamentalist Circumcision Party had carried the day with a literalistic interpretation of scripture, we would probably have had no more Tituses or Corneliuses in the community. Such an interpretation of scripture would have limited the salvific intent of God, which is after all what scripture is really about. Perhaps Eugene LaVerdiere best describes how people like Titus and Cornelius get sacrificed when we don't take into account the human limitations of the Bible:

> When human beings act on a Word which they judge to be purely divine, they may engage in actions which common sense and decency label as inhuman. With a lopsided view of the divinity of the Word, we can easily think of ourselves as divine, and our divine Word becomes an inhuman word.

We're Fundamentalists, Too

In the preceding section we have contrasted the fundamentalist and Catholic approaches to the Bible. Obviously, we prefer the Catholic approach. But we must acknowledge that at times we ourselves and our church have also used the fundamentalist approach. We have already given examples of our own fundamentalism, such as our acceptance of Father Doyle's threats of hell based upon his interpretation of scripture. In our Church, one example is that in the early 1900s the Pontifical Biblical Commission, an official organ of the Roman Catholic Church, taught with binding authority that the authors of the Gospel of Matthew and the Gospel of John were two of the twelve apostles. In 1955, that same Commission reversed itself and gave Catholics permission to freely express other views about the authorship of the Gospels and other books of the Bible.

A fundamentalist mindset has led the Catholic Church to make other hurtful decisions regarding entire groups of people, such as Jews and slaves, as well as individuals, such as Galileo. As the Spirit that guides the Church continues to reveal salvific truth in everyday life experience, hopefully we will follow in the footsteps of Peter and Paul and discover other areas of fundamentalist thinking in ourselves and in our Church.

Healing Process

1. Close your eyes, place your hand on your heart and breathe deeply. Recall a time when a passage of scripture was interpreted to you in a way that made it an "inhuman word," a word that was not consistent with "common sense and decency."

2. Imagine yourself at the Council of Jerusalem. The question of circumcision has been resolved, and you ask the participants if they will stay a little longer to help you. Read to them the passage of scripture and share the interpretation that has been given to you. Ask Paul, Peter, James and the others to listen to the Spirit with you as you seek a loving interpretation.

3. Let the conversation unfold in your imagination until all of you come to an agreement that resonates with what you know of common sense and your experience of giving and receiving love. Ask Paul, Peter and James to intercede that the "Spirit that is a living aid in ongoing interpretation" will continue revealing to you and the entire Church the salvific truth contained in this passage.

CHAPTER 8

Life Is Revelation

The Council of Jerusalem ended as it did because the participants heard God not only through scripture but also through life. God spoke to Paul and Peter through their life experience of Titus and Cornelius. Scripture affirms that God dwells within each person and within all of life in a non-violent and life-giving way. Much of the "messiness" of the Bible is precisely because it does incorporate all of life, including those places where the indwelling presence of God has become obscured (wars, adulteries, etc.). It also includes everyday examples such as seeds growing, a woman baking bread, and such. The point is that *everything* is a burning bush. The biblical authors went through a process of coming to understand this, taking three steps forward and two steps backward.

The modern theologian Dick Westley expresses well why we, like Paul and Peter, can hear God in all of life:

> It is wisely said, "Experience is the best teacher." . . . The primary and most obvious reason for this is that revelation is not over, God is constantly revealing himself to us in our experience. . . . Of course, the Bible is divine revelation—no one denies that. *But so is life!* It is precisely because God is present to life and available to human experience that *we* have a divinely inspired story to tell, and that the story once told is revelation.

In recent years, many people have discovered, as Peter and Paul did, that their life experience is revelatory of God. One source of this discovery in the Roman Catholic Church, beginning in the late 1960s after Vatican II, has been the explosion of houses of prayer, prayer groups, and faith-sharing

groups. Participants in all of these settings gather to share their own life experience of God. Like Paul and Peter, they give testimonies of how, through a conversation with a friend, a moment with nature or in some other everyday occurrence, God has revealed God's self to them in a powerful way. These groups have been part of a dramatic shift in the Catholic Church. This shift is away from an emphasis upon external authority to an emphasis upon internal authority. "Ordinary" laypeople now feel free to say, "This is what God within seems to be revealing to me."

This shift in the Roman Catholic Church reflects a paradigm shift throughout our entire culture that began around 1968. Previously, we tended to assume that authorities were right. Since then, we tend increasingly to suspect that they might be wrong. The historical reasons for this shift include the Vietnam War, Vatican II, Watergate, the feminist movement, democratically oriented parenting programs, the civil rights movement, twelve-step recovery and other consciousness movements and the findings of modern physics suggesting that everyone and everything participates in the same infinite consciousness that created the universe. Such events have made it clear to the general population that government and church authorities as well as doctors, lawyers, etcetera can make mistakes and often need to be challenged. Laypeople now tend to place more trust in their own inner authority. An authoritarian model is giving way to a mutuality/partnership model.

Jesus Started the Paradigm Shift

Although this shift may seem revolutionary to those who are living through it, it actually began with Jesus. As theologian Brother David Steindl-Rast says, it is

> . . . today's ripple of what happened when the stone was thrown into the pond two thousand years ago. It took that long for us to feel these ripples of the authority problem, because with Jesus a totally different view of authority came in. . . . Where did Jesus locate the divine authority? There is first the possibility that Jesus would have, like all the prophets did, located the divine authority behind himself: "God's authority stands behind me and thus says the Lord." Every prophet comes with this stance. . . . At first, they did call Jesus a prophet. . . . But that title didn't

stick. And why didn't it stick? Because Jesus, precisely with regard to authority, had a totally different attitude than the prophets. He did not locate the divine authority behind him.

. . . Another possibility would be, and the Gospel according to John suggests that very strongly, that he located the divine authority within himself. . . . Yes, to a certain extent that is true, but. . . . historically that cannot have been as pronounced as it appears in John. . . . Jesus did not go around and say, "I have all the answers. Listen to me. All the authority is invested in me. I am the way and the truth and the life." . . . Where did he locate the divine authority? In the hearts of his hearers.*

---

*In the Gospel of John, Jesus does say, "I am the way and the truth and the life" (John 14:6), and in many other passages John presents Jesus as locating the divine authority within himself. However, most scripture scholars agree that this is true theologically but not historically. In other words, the Gospel of John is not a historically accurate record of what Jesus said, but rather theological reflection on how Jesus lived. Jesus lived so that it is true to say of him that he is the way, the truth and the life, even though he probably did not say this of himself.

One way Jesus located divine authority in the hearts of his hearers was through parables, his usual way of teaching. He typically began his parables with words that imply, "Who of you doesn't already know this?" He used ordinary images from the daily lives of the people (a parent with a hungry child, a wedding feast, a shepherd who has lost a sheep, etc.), to show how God is always revealing God's self to them in everyday experiences. His parables are a way of encouraging his listeners to reflect on their own lives as a way of bringing to consciousness the revelation that they already know. One message of the parable is, "So, you know it already. Good! Well, do it." Thus, rather than drawing authority to himself, Jesus encouraged people to trust their own experience. He communicated, "God's authority stands behind *you*."

We (Dennis and Sheila) experience this every night when our son, John, curls up beside us in our bed. As we tenderly hold him and watch him sleeping, we know as never before the salvific truth of the Bible that God loves us infinitely:

> Can a woman forget her nursing child,
> or show no compassion for the child of her womb?
> Even these may forget, yet I will not forget you. (Isa 49:15)

We must admit that these words of scripture did not fully convey the love of God to us until we had our own child and realized that our love for him is a glimpse of how God loves us. For us, our son, John, is now our primary source of revelation, and it is in light of our love for him that we understand the salvific message of the Bible. Since Jesus knows this about us, we suspect that if he were preaching in our neighborhood today, he would tell us a parable about the love of parents for their child.

Jesus' trust of the experience of his hearers and his empowerment of their inner authority was a threat to the religious and political authorities of his time. The threat was so great that those structures put him to death. From his limited point of view, Caiaphas was right: It was "better for one man to die" (John 18:14) than for the whole system to fall apart. *Comunidades de base* (Base Christian Communities) in Latin America provide a modern parallel. In these communities the poor and disempowered have come together in prayer and faith-sharing groups. They, too, reflect on how God is revealing God's self to them through their life experience. As they

have recovered their own inner authority, they also have become a threat to the religious and political authorities. Like Jesus, tens of thousands have been put to death by the system they have challenged.

All *of Life Is Revelation*

Jesus trusted not only the authority within persons, but he also trusted nature and all of life as revelatory. In his parables, he encouraged his followers to find revelation in the most ordinary experiences of life. He often refers to nature as a source of revelation: birds of the air, lilies of the field, mustard seeds, leaven and so forth. Thus, St. Thomas Aquinas could say that there are two sources of revelation: scripture and nature.

Aquinas trusted the use of human reason to explore nature, and it seems that modern physics is repaying Aquinas's trust by its increasing recognition of the spiritual foundation of the universe. Many highly regarded physicists are now suggesting that the same loving presence apprehended in the most advanced stages of prayer is at the heart of all creation. We are not made from distinct atoms unconnected to each other, as the Newtonian worldview implied. Rather, all of creation is one and is a manifestation of a single, universal consciousness that created and continues to create us and the entire universe.

It seems that consciousness does not, as once thought, emerge from matter as if by accident. Rather, today many scientists would say that consciousness is the essential and original stuff of the universe and matter is a rather superficial crust upon this vast sea of consciousness. Everything indwells within that universal consciousness, and that universal consciousness indwells everything. Teilhard de Chardin called this universal consciousness love or God. Thus, the growing number of scientists who posit a universal consciousness are offering a possible explanation of how God indwells everything. In other words, the findings of science are increasingly consistent with the fundamental theme of the Bible: God indwells all of life. The image of Jesus' descent into hell is all the more meaningful in light of modern physics: There is no place where God is not.

The founder of the Jesuit order, St. Ignatius of Loyola, understood this. When Ignatius wanted to experience God's love, he would watch the stars at night. The stars filled him with awe and reminded him that the same God who made those stars was caring for him. Such experiences led to the spiritual tradition he founded, based upon "finding God in all things." *The Spiritual Exercises of St. Ignatius* is the guide St. Ignatius wrote for those who wanted to follow this tradition. The *Exercises* help us discover the revelation of God in nature and in every life experience.

The primary way Ignatius recommended for doing this was a simple process known as the examen. For many years, we have ended each day by sharing the examen together. We light a candle, become aware of God's loving presence, and take about five minutes of quiet while we each ask ourselves two questions:

For what moment today am I most grateful (what was my moment of
    consolation)?
For what moment today am I least grateful (what was my moment of
    desolation)?

There are many other ways to ask the same questions:

How is God indwelling in my life today?
How am I missing God's indwelling in my life today?

When did I give and receive the most love today?
When did I give and receive the least love today?

When did I feel most alive today?
When did I most feel life draining out of me?

When did I have the greatest sense of belonging to myself, others, God
    and the universe?
When did I have the least sense of belonging?

When was I happiest today?
When was I saddest?

Then we share these two moments with each other. Usually the entire
process takes about twenty minutes. When we are tired, we can easily finish
in ten.

The questions get us in touch with two movements that Ignatius calls consolation and desolation. By *consolation*, Ignatius meant whatever leads us to greater faith, hope and love. In modern language, we would say that consolation is whatever helps us feel more connected to ourselves, others, God and the universe. By *desolation*, Ignatius meant whatever leads us away from faith, hope and love (whatever disconnects us from ourselves, others, God and the universe). He believed that by paying attention to these two movements within us, we would come to know what the voice of God within us most wanted to reveal.

As Jesus interpreted the Bible, he seems to have paid attention to these same two movements. For example, as we have said, he quotes certain parts of the law that are more consistent with love and avoids other parts that seem inconsistent with love. If in a particular situation he can't find something loving in the Bible about it, then he says or does something new that is consistent with love. Later Matthew, Paul and the Council of Jerusalem seem to have done something similar. Jesus encouraged us to follow this example and get in touch with the wisdom within us when he so often says, in effect, "Who of you doesn't already know this?"

Thus, the examen is a way of living according to the underlying theme of the Bible, by helping us discover revelation—the burning bush—in everyday life. The Bible is a record of a people reflecting upon how God indwells their life experience. The examen is a simple method for doing this.

The Examen Gives Us Radar for Salvific Truth

For many years, when I (Sheila) did the examen I noticed a consistent pattern to what gave me consolation and desolation. My moments of consolation centered around children. For example, at the end of a travel day, I would typically be most grateful for the times I played with a child at the airport while waiting for a plane. Such moments confirmed my lifelong desire for a child. My moments of desolation were whenever having a child seemed impossible: medical tests indicating it was not likely that Denny could father a child; times when our ministry schedule was especially demanding and we wondered whether we could care for a child; days when I felt overwhelmed by fears that I would be as inadequate a parent as my own mentally ill mother.

Most discouraging of all were the times when well-meaning friends quoted scriptures to me about accepting God's will. They implied that it was obvious I wasn't going to have a child and I should give up trying. Such scriptures filled me with a fundamental sense of desolation. Although I really tried, I could not hear God speaking to me through them.

I considered that perhaps I was blocked by hurts and not free to hear God's will, and I sought healing with the help of a spiritual director and a counselor. They assured me that I was listening well, and they encouraged me in my longing for a child.

My experience raises another issue to consider in reading scripture: Although a passage of scripture may sound loving in general, it still may not be what God wishes to say to me at this particular moment in my life. The scriptures my friends quoted to me were interpreted in a way that was consistent with a loving image of God, yet the desolation I felt when I read them meant that they were not God's loving word for *me*, in my situation at that moment.

The one scripture that most felt like God's loving word for me during this time was the angel's words to Mary regarding her cousin Elizabeth's pregnancy: "For nothing will be impossible with God" (Luke 1:37). The consolation I felt when I read this matched the pattern of consolation in my life experience, in which moments of playing with a child most revealed God's love to me. Thus, I set aside other passages and read Luke 1:37 every day as we waited for John. When he finally came, I knew *those* were the words God had been speaking to me.

Doing the examen gave me a radar for how God was speaking to me in all of life, including in the scriptures. It helped me avoid relating to scripture in such a way that it "becomes an inhuman word." If I had accepted an interpretation of scripture that suggested I should give up the deepest calling of my life—to be a mother—the words of scripture would have been cruel and inhuman for me. On the other hand, Luke 1:37 was salvific truth for me at that time in my life.*

---

*What if there had been no child coming to me? What if, like my friend, Amy, I had always wanted a child but never had one? When I look at Amy's life, I see that she is at peace (although not without having passed through several years of struggle). My guess is that the very passages about accepting God's will that were desolation for me would be consolation for her. Perhaps she would experience them not only as loving in general, but the specific words of love she needed for her life situation.

When our radar for salvific truth is developed through practices like the examen, we may not always know what a scripture *does* mean, either in general or for us in particular, but we will more likely know what it does *not* mean. For example, I (Dennis) recall a conference at which we shared some of the ideas presented in this book. A participant asked, "How does what you've told us help me read the Book of Revelation?" He then quoted one of the more frightening passages in Revelation in a confrontive tone that communicated, "Now I've got you!" Underlying his angry voice, I sensed fear in him, which then seemed to reverberate around the room. I, too, began to feel afraid, and I fumbled to answer. I could not think clearly and forgot what I know from scripture scholarship about the importance of not interpreting Revelation literalistically.

The fear in the questioner, in the group and in myself is a sign that all of us were disconnected from our radar for salvific truth. The examen could have helped us. The fear in the room was desolation because it was contrary to "faith, hope and love." Instead of trying to answer the questioner directly, I could have helped him compare this desolation with his moments of consolation.

For example, I might have asked him to recall moments of consolation with the person who loves him the most. Then I could have asked him if that person would threaten him with the punishments suggested by a literalistic reading of the Book of Revelation. I would have assured him that God would treat him at least as lovingly as that person. Finally, I would have said that although he might not know what the Book of Revelation *is* saying to him, he can know that God is *not* saying anything that contradicts his experience of love.

Healing Process

Following is the examen process we use each day as a way of helping us develop our radar for the voice of God in scripture as well as in everyday life. Our hope is that it will help you know from within what is salvific truth for you and what is not.

1. You may wish to light a candle. Do whatever helps you to experience unconditional love. For example, imagine yourself in a favorite place with someone whose love you trust, such as a friend, Jesus or God as you understand God. Put your feet flat on the floor, take a few deep breaths from the bottom of your toes, up through your legs, your abdominal muscles and your chest. Breathe in that unconditional love and when you breathe out, fill the space around you with it.

2. Place your hand on your heart and ask Jesus or God as you understand God to bring to your heart the moment today for which you are most grateful. If you could relive one moment, which one would it be? When were you most able to give and receive love today?

3. Ask yourself what was said and done in that moment that made it so special. Breathe in the gratitude you felt and receive life again from that moment.

4. Ask God to bring to your heart the moment today for which you are least grateful. When were you least able to give and receive love?

5. Ask yourself what was said and done in that moment that made it so difficult. Be with whatever you feel without trying to change or fix it in any way. You may wish to take deep breaths and let God's love fill you just as you are.

6. Give thanks for whatever you have experienced. If possible, share as much as you wish of these two moments with a friend.

You may wish to apply this examen process to your reading of scripture as you consider a possible interpretation:

1. Recall typical moments of consolation in your life.

2. Recall typical moments of desolation in your life.

3. Does the interpretation you are considering match the growth in faith, hope and love (connection with yourself, others, God and the universe) that you experience in moments of consolation? If so, then this is probably part of God's salvific truth for you.

    4. Or, does it more closely match the diminishment of faith, hope and love (disconnection from yourself, others, God and the universe) that you experience in moments of desolation? If so, then this interpretation is probably not part of God's salvific truth for you. Although you may not yet know what the passage does mean, you have a clue as to what it does not mean.

Notes

Preface

Page vi: For physics and the wholistic nature of the universe, see John Hagelin, "Quantum Physical Foundations of Higher States," audiocassette of presentation at the International Conference on Science and Consciousness, Albuquerque, April 1999 (Santa Fe: The Message Co., 1999).

Chapter 1

Page 6: For the history of the Catholic Church's teaching regarding slavery, see Philip Kaufmann, *Why You Can Disagree and Remain a Faithful Catholic* (New York: Crossroad, 1989), pp. 21–25.

Page 7: For the use of *ʿezer* in the Old Testament, see John H. Otwell, *And Sarah Laughed* (Philadelphia: Westminster Press, 1977), p. 17.
James Fischer, *Interpreting the Bible* (Mahwah, N.J.: Paulist Press, 1986), p. 81.

Chapter 2

Page 11, footnote: Karl Rahner, ed., *Sacramentum Mundi: An Encyclopedia of Theology*, vol. 1 (New York: Herder & Herder, 1968), "Apocatastasis."

Page 13: Richard Rohr, audiocassette series *New Great Themes of Scripture*, tape # 1: "In the Beginning Is the End" (Cincinnati: St. Anthony Messenger Press, 1999).
Walter Wink, *Engaging the Powers* (Minneapolis: Fortress, 1992), p. 135.

Pages 13–14: Bernard Prusak, "Heaven and Hell: Eschatological Symbols of Existential Protest," *Cross Currents* (Winter 1975), pp. 481–82.

Page 14: Walter Wink, op. cit., p. 135.

Pages 14, 16: Personal letter from Susan Mech. Used with the author's permission.

Page 16: Raymond Brown, *An Introduction to the New Testament* (New York: Doubleday, 1997), p. 22.

Page 17: Dennis Hamm, S.J., "The Real Messianic Secret," *America*, 181:15 (November 13, 1999), pp. 30–31.

Pages 18–19 : Regarding Von Balthasar's understanding of the descent into hell, see John R. Sachs, S.J., "Universal Salvation and the Problem of Hell," *Theological Studies*, 52 (1991), pp. 242–46, and the Jerusalem Bible (Garden City, N.Y.: Doubleday, 1966), 495, footnote h. See also Elizabeth Johnson, *Consider Jesus* (New York: Crossroad, 1994), pp. 138–39. Quote from Von Balthasar on page 26 is a translated excerpt from "Abstieg zur Holle," quoted in *The Von Balthasar Reader*, Medard Kehl and Werner Loser, eds. (New York: Crossroad, 1982), p. 153, cited in Sachs, op. cit., p. 244. Von Balthasar continues:

> . . . the one who has timelessly closed himself off is opened up through the inescapable presence of another, who is just as timelessly near him and calls his presumptuous, seeming unapproachability into question.

Karl Rahner says something similar in his autobiographical interview:

> . . . if a people or even humanity were to fall into the abyss, then I would still be firmly convinced—and I hope to keep this conviction—that even such an abyss always ultimately ends in the arms of an eternally good, eternally powerful God. (*I Remember* [New York: Crossroad, 1985], p. 111)

Page 19: This story of a mother who asks to enter hell is from Leslie Weatherhead, *The Christian Agnostic* (New York: Abingdon, 1965), p. 274.

Page 20: Barclay writes:

> The Greek word of punishment is *kolasis*, which was not originally an ethical word at all. It originally meant the pruning of trees to make them grow better. I think it is true to say that in all Greek secular literature, *kolasis* is never used of anything but remedial punishment. The word for eternal is *aionios*. It means more than everlasting, for Plato—who may have invented the word— plainly says that a thing may be everlasting and still not be *aionios*. A simple way to put it is that *aionios* cannot be used properly of anyone but God; it is the word uniquely, as Plato saw it, of God. Eternal punishment is then literally that kind of remedial punishment which it befits God to give and which only God can give.

See William Barclay, *A Spiritual Autobiography* (Grand Rapids: Eerdmans, 1975), pp. 58–61. Not all lexicons and commentaries agree with Barclay's definition of *kolasis*. One commentary that does agree is Grundy's, in which he says that the Aramaic equivalent in Daniel 12 does refer to pruning. See Robert H. Grundy, *Matthew: A*

Commentary on His Handbook for a Mixed Church Under Persecution, 2nd ed. (Grand Rapids: Eerdmans, 1994), p. 516.

Paul certainly does emphasize the seriousness of turning away from God and the condemnation this warrants (e.g., Rom 2:5–8; 1 Cor 6:9–10; 2 Cor 5:10; 2 Thess 1:5–9; Phil 3:19). However, he never affirms that any human being, given the love and mercy of God, does actually permanently turn away. In other words, his statements may be taken as warnings, not as descriptions of actual future events. Overall, in Paul's thinking, "human sin is seen as explicable only as a stage on the way towards the triumph of God's grace." (William J. Dalton, S.J., *Salvation and Damnation* [Theology Today Series #41] [Butler, Wis.: Clergy Book Service, 1977], p. 44.) Thus Paul can say, "God has imprisoned all in disobedience so that he may be merciful to all" (Rom 11:32).

A scripture that is sometimes cited to prove that there *are* people in hell, or that once a person gets to hell he or she cannot leave, is the story of the rich man and Lazarus, in Luke 16:19–31. Lazarus, a poor beggar, dies and goes to heaven where he is in the bosom of Abraham. The rich man, who had not reached out to help Lazarus, dies and goes to hell. The rich man asks if he can go back and warn his five brothers so that they will not end up in hell too. Abraham refuses.

A clue that this story is not what it appears to be, that is, that it is not to be taken literally as proof that some people are in an eternal state of hell, is the rich man's desire to help others and Abraham's refusal to permit it. If we define heaven as a state of giving and receiving love, and hell as a state of total alienation in which no love is given or received and repentance is impossible, then the compassionate, unselfish, repentant rich man is at this point behaving more like a resident of heaven than is Abraham. A possible interpretation of the story is as follows: First, social standing in this world can be turned upside down in the next. Secondly, if you ignore your brothers and sisters in need (as the rich man did previously), you will feel like hell. (Cf. Esteban Deak, *Apokatastasis: The Problem of Universal Salvation in Twentieth-Century Theology* [Esteban Deak: Toronto, 1979, ISBN # 0969011504], pp. 296–97, 303; Dalton, op. cit., p. 37.)

For a discussion of other passages in the New Testament that are cited to prove that there are people in hell, see Dalton, op. cit. Although Dalton does deal with each of the most commonly cited passages, as he points out, it is not ultimately helpful to argue one passage against another. Fundamental theological issues, such as human salvation, must be understood, not on the basis of individual texts, but in light of the core message of the Gospel.

Pages 22–23: William Wilson, "A Monk's Prayer as Parent Radically Different," *Bread Rising*, 9:3 (April 1999), p. 3. Used with the author's permission.

Page 23: For summary of research on altruism in young children, see Sharon Begley and Claudia Kalb, "Learning Right from Wrong," *Newsweek* (March 13, 2000), pp. 30–33.

Page 24: Richard F. Smith, S.J., "Inspiration and Inerrancy," in *The Jerome Biblical Commentary*, vol. 2, edited by Raymond E. Brown, S.S., Joseph A. Fitzmyer, S.J. and Roland E. Murphy, O. Carm. (Englewood Cliffs, N.J.: Prentice-Hall, 1968), p. 502.

   Rohr, op. cit.

   Eugene LaVerdiere, S.S.S., "Fundamentalism and the Bible," p. 15 (unpublished paper presented at the Diocesan Liaisons' Theological Symposium in Plymouth, Michigan, in September 1987), cited in Theodore Dobson, *Catholic and Fundamentalist Approaches to the Bible* (Lakewood, Colo.: Easter Publications, 1988), p. 13.

Chapter 3

Page 27: Walter Wink, op. cit., p. 268.

Page 28: Walter Wink, op. cit., p. 269.

Page 29: Jerome Neyrey, S.J., "A Symbolic Approach to Mark 7," *Foundations and Facets Forum*, 4:3 (September 1988), pp. 82–83.

Pages 30–31: Joseph Fitzmyer, S.J., in *Anchor Bible: The Gospel According to Luke*, X–XXIV, vol. 28a (Garden City, N.Y.: Doubleday, 1985), #108: "On Divorce," p. 1120, and Joseph Fitzmyer, "The Matthean Divorce Texts and Some New Palestinian Evidence," *Theological Studies*, 37:2 (June 1976), pp. 213–21.

Chapter 4

Page 36: Dennis Hamm, S.J., "Preaching Biblical Justice," *Studies in the Spirituality of Jesuits*, 29:1 (January 1997), p. 25.

   Walter Wink, op. cit., p. 210.

Pages 39–40: Our interpretation of Luke 19:11–27 was originally inspired by James Lockman, O.F.M., "Re-examining the Parable of the Pounds" (unpublished paper, Graduate Theological Union, Berkeley, Calif.). See also Megan McKenna, *Parables: The Arrows of God* (Maryknoll, N.Y.: Orbis, 1994), pp. 118–21.

   Regarding usury, see Marcus Borg, *Jesus: A New Vision* (San Francisco: Harper, 1987), p. 96.

   See The Jerusalem Bible (Garden City, N.Y.: Doubleday, 1966), p. 125, noted.

Page 40: On the meaning of the cross, see John Dominic Crossan, *Jesus: A Revolutionary Biography* (San Francisco: Harper, 1994), pp. 125–28, and "Faith and Terror," *Sojourners* (September/October 1996), p. 39.

Pages 42–44, 46–48: Walter Wink, op. cit., pp. 175–94. Quote on our p. 46 is from Wink, p. 179.

Chapter 5

Page 50: Richard Rohr, O.F.M., "Biblical Roots of Mercy," presentation at the conference of the Association of Christian Therapists, September 1988.

Page 52: Source for the story about God's response to the drowning of the Egyptians is the Babylonian Talmud, Megillah 10b and Sanhedrin 39b.
    Source for the rabbis' interpretation of Leviticus 18:5 is Charles Krauthammer, "Demystifying Judaism," *Time* (August 21, 2000), p. 38.

Page 53: On violence in the Old Testament, see Wink, op. cit., p. 146.

Page 54: Robert Jewett, *Jesus Against the Rapture* (Philadelphia: Westminster Press, 1979), pp. 51–65; quote is from p. 55.

Page 55: On the shift away from purity and toward compassion, see Marcus Borg, *Meeting Jesus Again for the First Time* (San Francisco: Harper, 1994), pp. 50–58.
    Walter Wink, op. cit., p. 209.

Chapter 6

Pages 60–62: Jerome Neyrey, S.J., *Christ Is Community: The Christologies of the New Testament* (Collegeville, Minn.: Michael Glazier, 1985), pp. 65–104.

Page 60: Raymond E. Brown, *Responses to 101 Questions on the Bible* (Mahwah, N.J.: Paulist Press, 1990), p. 56.

Page 61: Austin P. Flannery, O.P., ed., *The Documents of Vatican II* (New York: Pillar, 1975), #58: "Dogmatic Constitution on Divine Revelation," #19, p. 761.

Chapter 7

Page 64: Raymond E. Brown, *An Introduction to the New Testament* (New York: Doubleday, 1997), p. 306.

Pages 67–71: On the difference between fundamentalist and Catholic approaches to the Bible, see the pamphlet by Eugene LaVerdiere, S.S.S., *Fundamentalism: A Pastoral Concern* (Collegeville: Liturgical Press, 1983); Dobson, op. cit.; Richard McBrien, *Catholicism* (San Francisco: Harper, 1994), pp. 59–66, 93–95, 105–06, 1194; National Conference of Catholic Bishops' Ad Hoc Committee on Biblical Fundamentalism, *A Pastoral Statement for Catholics on Biblical Fundamentalism*, March 26, 1987.

Page 68: Quote regarding fundamentalism is from National Conference of Catholic Bishops' Ad Hoc Committee on Biblical Fundamentalism, op. cit., p. 1.

Richard McBrien, op. cit., p. 63.

Page 69: Richard Smith, op. cit., p. 502.

On the authorship of the Gospels as coming from the traditions of various communities rather than eyewitness accounts, see Raymond E. Brown, *Responses to 101 Questions on the Bible*, p. 59.

Footnote: Richard McBrien, op. cit., pp. 62–63.

Quote regarding the gospel writers lack of concern for "uncolored factuality," from Raymond E. Brown, *Responses to 101 Questions on the Bible*, p. 56.

Page 70: On the shift in Matthew regarding the Gentiles, see Jerome H. Neyrey, S.J., "Decision Making in the Early Church: The Case of the Canaanite Woman (Matt 15:21–28)," *Science et Esprit*, 33:3 (1981), pp. 373–78.

National Conference of Catholic Bishops' Ad Hoc Committee on Biblical Fundamentalism, op. cit., p. 3.

Page 71: Quote regarding the Spirit as "a living aid in ongoing interpretation," is from Raymond E. Brown, *An Introduction to the New Testament*, p. 31.

Eugene LaVerdiere, *Fundamentalism: A Pastoral Concern*, p. 2.

On the Pontifical Biblical Commission and the authorship of Matthew and John, see Raymond E. Brown, *Responses to 101 Questions on the Bible*, p. 59.

Chapter 8

Page 73: Dick Westley, *A Theology of Presence* (Mystic, Conn.: Twenty-Third Publications, 1988), pp. 29, 31, 35.

Page 75: On the paradigm shift beginning in 1968, see Denise Breton and Christopher Largent, *The Paradigm Conspiracy* (Center City, Minn.: Hazelden, 1996). See also Karl Rahner, S.J., "Towards a Fundamental Theological Interpretation of Vatican II," *Theological Studies*, 40:4 (December 1979), 716–27.

Pages 75–76: David Steindl-Rast, "Prayer in the 21st Century," audiotape published by Credence Cassettes/National Catholic Reporter, Kansas City, Mo., 1992.

Page 79: Regarding nature as a source of revelation, see Thomas Aquinas, *Sermons on the Two Precepts of Charity and the Ten Precepts of the Law* (1273), 6.5, p. 129, cited in Matthew Fox, *Sheer Joy* (San Francisco: Harper, 1992), p. 59. See also John F. Haught, "Not Just Cheering from the Sidelines," *Praying*, 59 (March–April, 1994), pp. 11–15.

Summary of ideas from physics on the primacy and universality of consciousness are from John Hagelin, op. cit. See also Brian Swimme's videotape series, *Canticle to the Cosmos* (Livermore, Calif.: Newstory Project, 1990), on how the same "fecund emptiness" that created the universe also indwells all creatures.

Louis J. Puhl, S.J., ed., *The Spiritual Exercises of St. Ignatius* (Chicago: Loyola University Press, 1951). See, for example, nos. 23 and 230 ff.

Page 80ff.: For a more complete discussion of the examen as applied to modern life, including family life, see Dennis Linn, Sheila Fabricant Linn and Matthew Linn, *Sleeping with Bread: Holding What Gives You Life* (Mahwah, N.J.: Paulist Press, 1995).

Page 81: Louis J. Puhl, op. cit., no. 316.

Suggested Bibliography

Bible Translations and Related Tools

Most scholars recommend the New Revised Standard Version and the New Jerusalem Bible as the best translations. A synopsis of the Gospels may also be helpful, in which the texts of the three Synoptic Gospels (Matthew, Mark and Luke), and John, when it is relevant, are given in parallel columns so they can be compared. See Kurt Aland, ed., *Synopsis of the Four Gospels*, English Edition (New York: United Bible Societies, 1982) and Burton H. Throckmorton, ed., *Gospel Parallels: A Synopsis of the First Three Gospels* (Nashville: Nelson, 1992).

General Guides to Reading the Bible

Lawrence Boadt, *Reading the Old Testament* (Mahwah, N.J.: Paulist Press, 1984).

Raymond E. Brown, *An Introduction to the New Testament* (New York: Doubleday, 1997).

Roger Haight, *Dynamics of Theology* (Mahwah, N.J.: Paulist Press, 1990).

Daniel Harrington, *How to Read the Gospels* (Hyde Park, N.Y.: New City Press, 1996).

Daniel Harrington, *Interpreting the New Testament* (Collegeville, Minn.: Liturgical Press, 1988).

———, *Interpreting the Old Testament* (Collegeville, Minn.: Liturgical Press, 1991).

Pontifical Biblical Commission, *The Interpretation of the Bible in the Church* (Washington, D.C.: U.S. Catholic Conference, 1994).

Sandra Schneiders, *The Revelatory Text: Interpreting the New Testament as Sacred Scripture* (San Francisco: HarperCollins, 1991).

Arthur Zannoni, *Tell Me Your Name: Images of God in the Bible* (Chicago: Liturgy Training Publications, 2000).

Commentaries

Raymond E. Brown, Joseph A. Fitzmyer and Roland E. Murphy, eds., *The New Jerome Biblical Commentary* (Englewood Cliffs, N.J.: Prentice-Hall, 1990).

Daniel Harrington, *Sacra Pagina* Series (Collegeville, Minn.: Liturgical Press, 1991).

Robert J. Karris and Diane Bergant, eds., *Collegeville Bible Commentary* (Collegeville, Minn.: Liturgical Press, 1989).

Jesus and the Gospels

Raymond E. Brown, *An Introduction to New Testament Christology* (Mahwah, N.J.: Paulist Press, 1994).

John P. Meier, *A Marginal Jew: Rethinking the Historical Jesus*, vols. 1 and 2 (New York: Doubleday, 1991, 1994).

Dictionaries/Encyclopedias

Paul J. Achtemeier, ed., *Harper's Bible Dictionary* (San Francisco: HarperCollins, 1996).

David Noel Freedman, ed., *Anchor Bible Dictionary* (New York: Doubleday, 1992).

Resources for Further Growth

Books

Remembering Our Home: Healing Hurts & Receiving Gifts from Conception to Birth (with William Emerson; 1999). Integrates Christian spirituality with Dr. Emerson's pioneering work in the field of prenatal and perinatal psychology. Hurts in the womb, beginning at conception, tend to form a kind of template or pattern upon which later hurts are layered. Later hurts thus become far more crippling than they otherwise might be. This book maps the experience of the baby from conception through birth and the impact of those experiences on later life. It will help readers experience healing for themselves, their clients/directees/patients and their children (including infants and unborn babies) of the earliest wounds. Includes games and healing processes that can be used by laypeople of all ages, as well as by professionals.

Healing the Purpose of Your Life (1999). Each of us comes into this world carrying with us a special purpose given us by God, what Agnes Sanford called our "sealed orders." When we follow our sealed orders, we become fully alive, resolve midlife crises and avoid burnout. This book is to help us discover our sealed orders and heal the obstacles to living them out.

Simple Ways to Pray for Healing (1998). This book contains the eight simple ways of praying for healing that we have returned to most often in our ministry and integrates spirituality with contemporary physics and psychology. These ways of praying are simple enough for small children, yet profound enough to touch sophisticated adults.

Don't Forgive Too Soon: Extending the Two Hands That Heal (1997). When we are hurt, we are tempted to either act as a passive doormat or to strike back and escalate the cycle of violence. We can avoid both of these temptations and find creative responses to hurts by moving through the five stages of forgiveness. In so doing, we discover the two hands of nonviolence: one hand that stops the person who hurt us and the other that reaches out, calms that person and offers new life. This book has healing processes so simple that children can use them.

Sleeping with Bread: Holding What Gives You Life (1995). A simple process—for individuals and for families and others to share—of reflecting on each day's consolation and desolation. This process can help us get in touch each day with both hurts and healing, guide our decisions and help us find the purpose of our life. Includes a question-and-answer section at the end. Especially recommended for family spirituality.

Good Goats: Healing Our Image of God (1994). We become like the God we adore. Thus, one of the easiest ways to heal ourselves and our society is to heal our image of God, so that we know a God who loves us at least as much as those who love us the most. Discusses whether God throws us into hell or otherwise vengefully punishes us, and the role of free will. Includes a question-and-answer section that gives the theological and scriptural foundation for the main text.

Healing Spiritual Abuse & Religious Addiction (1994). Why does religion help some people grow in wholeness, yet seem to make others become more rigid and stuck? Discusses religious addiction and spiritual abuse, and offers ways of healing the shame-based roots of these behaviors. Includes how spiritual abuse can also be sexually abusive and how scripture has often been used to reinforce religious addiction and spiritual abuse. Concludes with an image of healthy religion, in which we are free to do what Jesus would do.

Belonging: Bonds of Healing & Recovery (1993). Twelve-Step recovery from any compulsive pattern is integrated with contemporary spirituality and psychology. This book helps the reader discover the genius underneath every addiction. Defines addiction as rooted in abuse and as our best attempt to belong to ourselves, others, God and the universe. Recovery comes from finding a better way to belong.

Healing the Eight Stages of Life (1988). Based on Erik Erikson's developmental system, this book helps to heal hurts and develop gifts at each stage of life, from conception through old age. Includes healing ways our image of God has been formed and deformed at each stage.

Healing the Greatest Hurt (1985). Healing the deepest hurt most people experience, the loss of a loved one, by learning to give and receive love with the deceased through the Communion of Saints.

Praying with Another for Healing (1984). Guide to praying with another to heal hurts such as sexual abuse, depression, loss of a loved one, etcetera.

To Heal as Jesus Healed (with Barbara Shlemon Ryan; 1978, revised 1997). This book, also on praying with another, emphasizes physical healing, including the healing power of the Sacrament of the Sick.

Healing the Dying (with Mary Jane Linn; 1979). How the seven last words of Jesus can help us prepare for death . . . and also for life.

Healing Life's Hurts: Healing Memories through the Five Stages of Forgiveness (1978, revised 1993). Contains a thorough discussion of the five stages of dying and how they apply to the process of forgiveness. Integrates spirituality with the findings of psychosomatic medicine regarding forgiveness.

Healing of Memories (1974). A simple guide to inviting Jesus into our painful memories to help us forgive ourselves and others.

These and other books by the authors (except *To Heal as Jesus Healed*) may be ordered from Paulist Press, 997 Macarthur Blvd., Mahwah, N.J. 07430; phone: (800) 218-1903; fax: (800) 836-3161. *To Heal as Jesus Healed* may be ordered from Resurrection Press, P.O. Box 248, Williston Park, N.Y. 11596; phone (516) 742-5686; fax (516) 746-6872.

Tapes and Courses (for use alone, with a companion, or with a group)

Good Goats: Healing Our Image of God (1994). Two-part videotape to accompany book (see above).

Healing Our Image of God (1994). Set of two audiotapes that may be used to accompany the book *Good Goats: Healing Our Image of God* and/or *Healing Spiritual Abuse & Religious Addiction*.

Healing Spiritual Abuse & Religious Addiction (1994). Audiotapes to accompany book (see above).

Belonging: Healing & 12 Step Recovery (1992). Audio- or videotapes and a course guide to accompany book (see above), for use as a program of recovery.

Healing the Eight Stages of Life (1991). Tapes and a course guide that can be used with book (see above) as a course in healing the life cycle. Available in video and audio versions.

Praying with Another for Healing (1984). Tapes that can be used with book (see above). Book includes course guide, and tapes are available in video and audio versions. *Healing the Greatest Hurt* (see above) may be used as supplementary reading for the last five of these sessions, which focus on healing of grief for the loss of a loved one.

Dying to Live: Healing through Jesus' Seven Last Words (with Bill & Jean Carr; 1983). How the seven last words of Jesus empower us to fully live the rest of our lives. Tapes (available in video or audio versions) may be used with the book *Healing the Dying* (with Mary Jane Linn, 1979).

Audiotapes for all of these courses are available from Christian Video Library, 3914-A Michigan Ave., St. Louis, Mo. 63118; phone: (314) 865-0729; fax: (314) 773-3115.

Videotapes for all of these courses (except *Good Goats*) are also available from Christian Video Library. *Good Goats* may be purchased from Paulist Press, 997 Macarthur Boulevard, Mahwah, N.J. 07430; phone: (800) 218-1903 or (201) 825-7300; fax: (800) 836-3161.

Videotapes on a Donation Basis

To borrow any of the above videotapes, contact Christian Video Library (address and telephone above).

Spanish Books and Tapes

Several of the above books and tapes are available in Spanish. For information, contact Christian Video Library.

Retreats and Conferences

For retreats and conferences by the authors on the material in this book and on other topics in the resources listed above, contact Dennis, Sheila and Matthew Linn, c/o Re-Member Ministries, 3914-A Michigan Ave., St. Louis, Mo. 63118; phone: (970) 476-9235 or (314) 865-0729; fax: (970) 476-9235 or (314) 773-3115.

About the Authors

Dennis, Sheila and Matt Linn work together as a team, integrating physical, emotional and spiritual wholeness, having worked as hospital chaplains and therapists, and currently in leading retreats and spiritual companioning. They have taught courses on processes for healing in over fifty countries and in many universities and hospitals, including a course to doctors accredited by the American Medical Association. Dennis and Matt are the coauthors of eighteen books, the last thirteen coauthored with Sheila. These books have sold over a million copies in English and have been translated into more than twenty different languages. Dennis and Sheila live in Colorado with their son, John, and Matt lives in a Jesuit community in Minneapolis.

About the Illustrator

Francisco Miranda lives in Mexico City. In addition to illustrating *Good Goats, Healing Spiritual Abuse & Religious Addiction, Sleeping with Bread, Don't Forgive Too Soon, Simple Ways to Pray for Healing, Healing the Purpose of Your Life* and *Remembering Our Home*, he has also written and illustrated several children's books. He is a renowned artist and sculptor whose work has been widely exhibited.